WHY NOT TRUST THE TORIES?

ANDREW GODSELL

First published as *A History of the Conservative Party* 1989
Second edition 1990
Third edition *Why Not Trust the Conservatives?* 2015

This fourth edition published 2021 as an Amazon paperback

ISBN 9798533360951

Blog andrewgodsell.wordpress.com

Twitter @AndrewGodsell

YouTube Channel Andrew Godsell

The Author

Andrew Godsell was born during 1964, in Hampshire. After education at a nondescript comprehensive school, and a sixth form college, Andrew did not go to university. He worked for a series of banks, while launching a writing career. Following this Andrew has been employed as a civil servant and local government officer – he is currently with the National Health Service.

Andrew's *British History* covers events in our island across eight thousand years, from the Stone Age to Brexit. *The World Cup and International Football 1872-2016* and *Europe United: A History of the European Cup / Champions League* are comprehensive football chronicles, while *Planet Football* features biographical sketches of some of the greatest players. *The Life and Diaries of Samuel Pepys* is a study of the amazing diarist. *Obsessive Compulsive Asperger* appeals as an attempt at alternative autobiography. *Alice's Adventures in Fantasyland* is a modern re-telling of a nineteenth century tale. Andrew is also the editor of *Get the Tories Out!: Our Socialist Media Campaign*, a collection of essays by political activists. His writings on diverse subjects have appeared in magazines, an educational textbook, and on several websites. A contribution to textual accuracy led to an acknowledgement of Mr A Godsell in the Penguin Classics edition of *Dracula* by Bram Stoker.

Andrew was interviewed by the BBC at the 1990 World Cup finals, and ITV at the 2006 tournament. He featured in the book *Twenty Nights to Rock: Touring with the Boss* by Bill Tangen, an American sports writer, and fellow Bruce Springsteen fan. Andrew starred on the BBC's *Weakest Link* (2009). Membership of the Labour Party has included participation in several General Elections, and even more local Elections. Andrew's political commentary has been broadcast by the BBC (2016) and Sky (2017).

Contents

Preface

With bold ambition, I began writing *A History of the Conservative Party* on September 30 1985. As a member of the Labour Party, it seemed natural I should plunge into literature with a critical history of the Conservatives, despite being aged only 20, and lacking any experience of writing for publication. I drew inspiration from Antonio Gramsci and Aneurin Bevan, Socialists who contributed original works to political literature.

Antonio Gramsci was imprisoned by Benito Mussolini's Fascist dictatorship in Italy. After his arrest, Gramsci wrote to Tatiana, sister of his wife, Julia Schucht: "I am obsessed by the idea that I ought to do something for ever. I want, following a fixed plan, to devote myself intensively and systematically to some subject that will absorb me and give a focus to my inner life". This led to Gramsci writing the *Prison Notebooks* (between 1929 and 1935), which rank among the most profound political writings. Gramsci's theory of hegemony, by which a ruling class asserts and reinforces its position, along with his advocacy of ways that the working class can counter this, have been a massive influence on Socialist thinking and action.

Aneurin Bevan's *Why Not Trust the Tories?* was published in 1944, when victory for Britain, and her allies, in the Second World War was in sight. A Labour government took power in 1945, with a landslide election victory, and delivered the welfare state. The defining achievement of Labour was the National Health Service, with Bevan, a Marxist agitator, being the architect. The Conservatives voted against establishment of the NHS in Parliament, and have continued to undermine its principles.

At the time I started writing this book, Margaret Thatcher was Prime Minister. As a Labour Party activist, I have consistently battled against the Conservative Party. Besides standing as a local Election candidate on numerous occasions, there have been a series of General Election campaigns. My book about the Conservatives was first published in 1989, and has remained in print ever since, across several editions. There is now a new title, reflecting the continued legacy of Aneurin Bevan – *Why Not Trust the Tories?* As these words are written, on the 73rd anniversary of the founding of our NHS, for which I proudly work, the struggle against the Tories continues.

Andrew Godsell

Hampshire
July 5 2021

1 Rotten Boroughs

The Conservative Party was established in 1830, upon the ruins of the failing Tory Party, founded in the seventeenth century. The names Conservative and Tory have been interchangeable since the 1830s. The party and their allies were alternatively known as the Unionists, from 1886 to 1924. The terrible Tory story stretches back to the reign of King Charles II, whose lack of a legitimate son led to the Exclusion Crisis. Protestants in Parliament attempted to remove James, the Catholic brother of Charles, from the succession. The group pushing for Exclusion, a campaign commenced in 1678, were dubbed Whigs by their opponents. This referred to the Whiggamores, a Scottish Presbyterian group, active during the Civil War of the 1640s. The Whigs in turn started, during 1681, to call supporters of James by the name Tory. The original Tories were Catholic guerillas, unsuccessfully attempting to defend Ireland, in the early 1650s, from conquest by the English army of Oliver Cromwell. The Tories began as victims of English intervention in Ireland, but were destined to become villains in the history of the latter country many times in the future. Both Whigs and Tories accepted the critical terms as a badge of honour, and many members of Parliament quickly became loyal to one of these embryo political parties.

James became the monarch, as James II, in 1685, but was deposed in 1688. For several decades, Jacobite supporters, and descendants, of James, who died in 1701, made consistent efforts to restore a Catholic monarchy, with backing from the Tories. The office of Prime Minister was effectively established in 1721, by Robert Walpole, a Whig, and his party were dominant through the rest of the eighteenth century. The Tory Party, having abandoned its Catholic roots to become a staunch defender of the Protestant constitution, gained strength during the early part of the nineteenth century. The government of Lord Liverpool held office for fifteen years, from 1812 to 1827. Liverpool was followed as Prime Minister by three more Tories, namely George Canning, who died in August 1827, Viscount Goderich, who resigned in January 1828, and then the Duke of Wellington. In 1815, Wellington had been leader of an international military force, which defeated France, at the Battle of Waterloo. His Tory government suffered a split, as the moderate Canningites, and reactionary Ultras, deserted. The Canningites were alienated by the government's support of electoral corruption in 1828, while the Ultras opposed to a law allowing Catholics to sit in Parliament, and take government office, passed in 1829. Catholic emancipation was carried at the instigation of Robert Peel, who led the government in the House of Commons.

The first recorded reference to a Tory metamorphosis, into the Conservative Party, appeared in the *Quarterly Review* of January 1830. An anonymous person wrote "We now are, as we always have been, decidedly and conscientiously attached to what is called the Tory, and which might with more propriety be called the Conservative Party". The usage grew over the following months, as an alternative to the Tory Party. The word Conservative originated in France. The Conservative Party, which prides itself on its essentially British nature, actually has a foreign name.

Wellington's government was able to remain in office as the opposition was divided – the latter being composed of the Whigs, the Radicals (a middle class party), the Canningites, and the Ultras. During 1830 Wellington faced calls for Parliamentary Reform, but the Tories were opposed, as they wished to maintain the political power of the landed elite. King George IV died in June, being succeeded by William IV, and a General Election followed in July. After the Election, the government felt able to regard 311 MPs as supporters, as against 347 opponents. Despite this defeat, Wellington announced, in November, that the government had no plans for Reform. Wellington claimed the present system of representation could not be improved, adding that he believed it possessed the "full and entire confidence of the country". The opposition united in the Commons to pass a motion to refer the civil list to a committee. Wellington responded to this display of a lack of confidence in his government by resigning. Lord Grey became Prime Minister, on November 22, leading a basically Whig administration, although it also included Radicals, Canningites, and Ultras.

A few days after the fall of Wellington's government, a number of his leading Parliamentary colleagues formed a committee, to organise the Conservative Party. Wellington and Peel played little part in the work of the committee, as they did not see politics in terms of parties, but thought in terms of service to the Crown. It was a sign of the lack of respect felt by the party for the committee that it was not even given a name.

The Whigs presented a Reform Bill to the House of Commons in March 1831. Although the proposals contained in the Bill would not alter the situation that only a tiny minority of the population enjoyed the franchise, they did represent a major change in the political structure of the nation. Whereas the existing electorate was dominated by the aristocracy, the Whigs planned to give the middle class an influence equal to that of the upper class. This was to be effected by a substantial reduction in the qualification for the franchise, which was based on wealth. The Bill proposed to abolish a large number of "rotten boroughs". These constituencies were largely controlled by the aristocracy – by means of bribery and intimidation of the electorate – in the interests of the Conservatives. There was some consolation for the Conservatives, as the Bill led to the Ultras rejoining the party.

In the Commons, Peel said the Bill was so radical it could not be improved by amendment, and that he would therefore pursue outright opposition. Peel declared that if the Bill was rejected there could be a civil war, but he did not seem to be troubled by this prospect. He argued that a civil war would be the fault of the Whigs for introducing the legislation. The Bill received its Second Reading, by one vote, in the early hours of March 23. The Conservatives inflicted a defeat on the government during the Committee stage, and Parliament was dissolved. At the General Election, in May 1831, the Conservatives won only 257 seats, whereas the combined forces of the Whigs and Radicals won 401 seats. This defeat prompted the formation of Conservative Associations in the constituencies to promote the party's cause.

A second Reform Bill was introduced in June. The government had no trouble in steering the Bill through the Commons, and it was passed in September. In October, the Bill was defeated by the Conservative majority in the Lords. The sequel was a series of demonstrations and riots throughout the country, with the working class joining the middle class in this agitation. The government introduced a third Reform Bill in December 1831, and this passed through the House of Commons without difficulty. The Conservatives' party committee established the Carlton Club, at Carlton Terrace in London, during March 1832. This served as a social and organisational centre. The party committee was disbanded a few months later, but its existence marked the beginning of extra-Parliamentary organisation in the Conservative Party, whereas the Tory Party had lacked anything of this type.

Conservative peers allowed the Reform Bill to receive its Second Reading in the Lords, during April, but proceeded to amend it in committee. The king would not allow the creation of enough new peers to prevent this, and the Whig government resigned in May. William IV sent for Lord Lyndhurst, who was the leading Ultra peer. Lyndhurst suggested that the king ask Wellington to form a government to carry Reform. Although opposed to Reform, Wellington agreed to take office in view of the national crisis. Wellington was unable to form a government, as the Conservatives were opposed to this course. The Whigs therefore returned to power a few days after their resignation. The king now persuaded the leading Conservative peers to allow the Bill to pass, to end the crisis, and gave the government a pledge to create as many peers as necessary in the event of obstruction. The Conservative peers relented, and the Bill received its Third Reading in the Lords on June 4.

The Reform Act set the franchise, restricted to men, and based on the annual rental value of buildings, at £10 in the boroughs, and £50 in the counties. Although their dominance had been ended, the aristocracy retained influence out of all proportion to their numbers. They had conceded some power to the middle class, but the working class remained unenfranchised. The Reform Act dealt only with England and Wales. Equivalent Acts for Scotland and Ireland were passed later in the year. Accepting the issue as settled, the Conservatives did not attempt to block the additional legislation. The government held a General Election on the new franchise, in December 1832, and were rewarded by the new voters, with a majority of 288 seats, as the combined forces of the Whigs and Radicals returned 473 MPs. The Conservatives suffered one of their worst ever electoral defeats, taking only 185 seats.

Faced with a new political framework, the Conservatives had to carefully consider their future direction. Acceptance of the word Conservative, in place of Tory, was a part of this process. The new name was readily taken up by the party, in an attempt to demonstrate that it was discarding its former approach, and making a fresh start, but the party maintained its defence of the ruling class. Although renamed the Conservative Party, it still referred to itself as the Tory Party. The ideas of the original Tories have continued to be influential. Edmund Burke, an eighteenth century MP and writer, has always been regarded by the Conservatives as an important thinker, despite the fact that he was a Whig for most of his life, only becoming a Tory in his final years. Burke eloquently expounded a reactionary viewpoint, but did not rely on pure resistance to change. He argued that, although continuity was favourable, society could only be maintained if there was scope for reform. Burke favoured limited change, in the interests of maintaining the basic structure of society. In the current era, he has been invoked by Theresa May, in a speech at the 2016 Party Conference, a few months into her premiership: "From Edmund Burke onwards, Conservatives have always understood that if you want to preserve something important, you need to be prepared to reform it. We must apply that same approach today. That's why where markets are dysfunctional, we should be prepared to intervene". In reality, May followed many other Conservative Prime Ministers, failing to tackle inevitable problems in the capitalist system.

The establishment of the Conservative Party on the basis of the Tory Party was not a move made out of choice, but as a reaction to necessity. This was appropriate, for the Conservative Party has always acted in response to necessity rather than out of positive wishes. The party emerged from the failure of its forerunner, and it has continued to practice a form of politics dominated by failure ever since. The party has set itself against progress, and has only accepted it when forced to do so. Whenever it has been successful in party terms, the Conservative Party has blocked progress, and thus failed the nation. Whenever the party has accepted progress, and thus benefitted the nation, it has done so as a result of the failure of its opposition to change.

In the period following the 1832 Election, the position of the Conservative Party gradually improved. It made gains at By-Elections, and within the House of Commons, as the government alienated moderate Whigs. In May 1834, several members of the government, led by Lord Stanley, resigned as they opposed lay appropriation of surplus revenues of the Irish Church. Lord Grey retired in July, being succeeded as Prime Minister by Lord Melbourne. In November, Melbourne insisted on the appointment of Lord John Russell, as Chancellor of the Exchequer, and Leader of the House of Commons. The king refused to accept Russell, who supported the lay appropriation policy. Melbourne offered his resignation, which the king accepted. In effect, the king had dismissed the government. Ernest Augustus, Duke of Cumberland and Teviotdale – a brother of William IV, and active Conservative member of the

House of Lords – had hopes of following this with a military coup, but decided against taking action. The king turned to Wellington, who agreed to be Prime Minister, on the understanding that he would hand over to Peel, when the latter returned from a visit to Rome.

Peel arrived back in London on December 9 1834, and set about forming a government. He wished to include Stanley and his supporters, but they declined to join the government, as they hoped to form a new party. Peel took the post of Chancellor of the Exchequer as well as Prime Minister, and Wellington was Foreign Secretary. Peel obtained a dissolution of Parliament, and a General Election was held in January 1835. Peel addressed the electors of his constituency, on behalf of the government, in the Tamworth Manifesto. Peel's ambivalent attitude to his party was demonstrated by the lack of any mention in the manifesto of the Conservative Party. Peel noted his moderate approach, but the manifesto did not set out any programme to be followed by the government. It was not a particularly impressive document but, in the absence of anything notably better, has assumed a hallowed place in the literature of the Conservative Party. In the constituencies the emerging Conservative Associations were active, but unable to match the traditional influence of bribery combined with the power of landowners. The Conservatives took 279 seats, but the combined forces of the Whigs and Radicals won 379 seats. The government's minority position in the Commons meant that it was ineffective. At the beginning of April, the opposition carried a motion in favour of Irish lay appropriation. This was the sixth defeat suffered by the government in as many weeks, prompting Peel to resign.

The Whigs returned to office, with Melbourne as Prime Minister. Following this, Stanley and his supporters gradually joined the Conservatives, having failed to form a new party. Peel believed the Conservatives should seek to maintain the traditional structure of the country, as far as was possible, by means of compromise, as opposed to resistance to change. Peel was a member of the capitalist class, and saw their interests as interdependent with the aristocracy. There was a major increase in the formation of Conservative constituency associations. This largely stemmed from a need to deal with the reality of the Reform Act, rather than any positive inclinations. The Conservative Party believed political activity should be limited to the narrow ranks of the wealthy, with the remainder of the population excluded. At the Carlton Club, which moved to a new building in Pall Mall in 1835, a committee was formed to deal with registration. The leading member of the committee was Francis Bonham, an assistant whip. Although he was not given an official position, Bonham was effectively the party's electoral agent.

In June 1837, William IV died, and was succeeded by Queen Victoria. A General Election, which followed in August, was won by the Whigs and the Radicals, with 344 seats, while the Conservatives had 314 MPs. In May 1839, the Whigs resigned, following a dispute with the Jamaican assembly. Peel agreed to take office but requested that, as a sign of confidence in the government, the queen should make changes in the composition of her household, which was dominated by women who were relatives of leading Whigs. The queen refused the request, and Peel responded by declining to take office. The queen recalled Melbourne, and the Whigs returned to office.

Peel was briefly troubled by a group called the Tory Radicals, whose name was a contradiction in terms, for Radicalism is the political antithesis of Toryism and Conservatism. The Tory Radicals thought the party's future lay in an alliance between the aristocracy and the working class, against the capitalists. This was not a realistic prospect, as working people did not have the vote. During the early part of 1841, Peel led a concerted attack on the government, aiming to bring about its downfall. This culminated on June 4, when Peel carried a Commons motion of no confidence, by one vote. Rather than resign, Melbourne gained a dissolution, and the Election was held in July. The Conservatives won 367 seats as against 291 for their opponents, which was a majority of 76, but Melbourne refused

to accept defeat. He met Parliament in August, and was forced
to resign, as the Conservatives carried an amendment to the
Address.

2 Two Nations

Robert Peel was appointed Prime Minister of a Conservative government, for the second time, in 1841. Wellington sat in the Cabinet, without holding departmental office, while Lord Stanley was Secretary for War and the Colonies. Peel signalled that he would put what he regarded as good government before party ties. The economy was in a troubled state, and free trade was an issue. The Conservative Party was overwhelmingly opposed to free trade, as a matter of principle, for it threatened the prosperity of the landed interest. On the other hand, Peel was prepared to consider it on its merits. Prior to the 1842 budget, Peel carried a Corn Law, which halved the protective scale of the 1828 equivalent, with Conservative MPs giving reluctant support. Peel introduced the budget himself rather than allowing the Chancellor, Henry Goulburn, to do so. The budget abolished a large number of duties on trade. Peel's support for capitalism, along with disregard for his party, increasingly alienated Conservatives. Dissatisfaction was reflected in the establishment, during 1843, of the Young England group, led by Benjamin Disraeli, who had established himself as a novelist before entering Parliament. Young England reflected the outlook of the Tory Radicals. Disraeli set out their ideas in two novels, *Coningsby, or, the New Generation* (1844) and *Sybil, or, the Two Nations* (1845). Disraeli was consistently critical of Peel in the Commons. On one occasion, Disraeli said Peel's actions demonstrated "that a Conservative government is an organised hypocrisy". Disraeli was one of the most talented Conservative MPs, but distrusted because he was so different from his colleagues. He was clever, of Jewish descent, and an adventurer.

Although increasingly troubled by rebellions from supporters, Peel was able to implement a second major Budget, in 1845, with a further large scale reduction of duties. This was followed by the Corn Law crisis. Peel believed that famine, stemming from failure of the Irish potato crop, required the removal of duties on imported grain. Peel already favoured free trade on general grounds, but was unable to reveal this, due to the views of his party. Lord Stanley – who had moved to the House of Lords in 1844 – advised Peel to suspend the Corn Laws, rather than repeal them. Peel declined the suggestion, and Stanley decided to resign from the government. This prompted Peel to offer his resignation, as Prime Minister, to Queen Victoria, in December 1845. The monarch asked Lord John Russell to form a government, but he was unable to sufficient support among the leading Whigs, and Peel returned to office. The Irish Famine lasted from 1845 until 1852, with the savage policies of both Conservative and Whig governments causing the death toll in Ireland to rise to around one million people, while another million people were forced to emigrate. With the British protestant ruling class concentrating on their own profits, landowners were cruelly exporting food from Ireland to Britain, while the Catholic working class starved. Nowadays the actions of the Conservatives and Whigs would be condemned as genocide and ethnic cleansing. Ireland had been forcibly incorporated by the United Kingdom in 1801, and the majority of the island remained under subjugation until gaining independence, in 1922. Since then the Conservatives, who fought a bitter campaign to maintain the Union with Ireland, have had a negative influence, as sectarian allies of Protestant politicians in Northern Ireland.

Peel hoped to carry repeal, and hold his party together, but regarded repeal as the more important consideration. Peel's plan provoked a split in the Conservative Party. The leaders of the revolt were Disraeli and another backbench MP, Lord George Bentinck. Peel announced the details of his proposals at the end of January 1846. They proved unacceptable to the Protectionists, who proceeded to form their own party. In February, Peel put forward a motion in the Commons in favour of repealing the Corn Laws. Peel secured a majority of 97 for the principle, but only due to support from the Whigs and Radicals, as most Conservatives opposed him. On March 8, a meeting elected

Lord Stanley, in his absence, the Protectionist Leader in the Lords. The Corn Law Bill received its Second Reading at the end of March, with a majority of 88, and this was followed by a 98 vote margin when the measure was carried on the Third Reading, in May. Bentinck was elected Leader of the Protectionists in the Commons, in late April, following which they planned to overthrow Peel. They decided to oppose his Irish Coercion Bill, despite agreeing with its aims. The Corn Law Bill received its Third Reading in the Lords on June 25. That same day, the Protectionists combined with the Whigs in the Commons, to defeat the Irish Coercion Bill by 73 votes. The Corn Law Act became law with Royal Assent on June 26, and Peel resigned on June 29.

The fact that the disputes over Peel's policies eventually split the party has always been regarded by the Conservatives as important. The Conservatives have been conscious of the need for unity, as the best way to defend their interests. This has led to a stifling of debate in the party. Although he was not held in high esteem at this point, Peel has come to be seen as one of the leading influences in the history of the Conservative Party. He developed what has come to be known as Peelism, the essence of which is a realistic approach to change. The party has learnt from Peel that, in order to be politically successful, it must not dogmatically resist change. Instead it has sought to follow Peel's lead, by accommodating itself to the inevitability of change. While defending the existing order of society, the Conservative Party has accepted that reforms are sometimes necessary, but only when the existing order begins to be untenable. In the Conservative view, change is required not as the implementation of ideals, but as a way of ensuring a functioning of society. The Conservative Party believes that its approach to reform is based on common sense, and that there is great value in people's attachment to the life with which they are familiar, and their consequent reservations about the unknown.

Peel's resignation, in 1846, was followed by the formation of a Whig government, with Lord John Russell as Prime Minister.

The Conservatives were in disarray. On July 8, the Duke of Richmond gave a dinner for the Protectionists, at which Bentinck said that he regarded Stanley as the overall Leader of the party. The Whigs were in a minority of around 80, but safe in office, with the two sections of Conservatives mainly intent on thwarting each other. Peel had no intention of retiring, or attempting to reunite the party. Despite Peel's lack of direction, he was still acknowledged as Leader by his supporters, with the group becoming known as the Peelites. In contrast to Peel, Stanley wished to reconstruct the party. Meanwhile Wellington retired from active politics.

The Whigs held a General Election in July 1847, and won 324 seats, ahead of the Protectionists, with 243 MPs, while 89 Peelites were returned. Although the divided forces of the Conservatives had won eight more seats than the Whigs, the latter retained power. The Protectionists gradually came to call themselves the Conservative Party, reverting to their previous name. Bentinck resigned as their Leader in the Commons, during December, following a dispute with the Chief Whip, William Beresford. This was caused by Bentinck's support for the admission of Jews to Parliament. The Conservative MPs did not find another Leader until February 1848, when the unimpressive Lord Granby was chosen. He found the task beyond him, and resigned after only three weeks. Following this, the Conservative MPs were leaderless, until a triumvirate Leadership was established in February 1849, composed of Disraeli, Granby, and J C Herries. Disraeli disregarded this awkward arrangement, choosing to act as though he were sole Leader in the Commons. Disraeli differed from the rest of his party, as he had a realistic view of its situation. Disraeli believed it was necessary to abandon Protection, as it was electorally disastrous. Stanley saw no point in active opposition to the government, given that his grouping would be unable to form an administration of their own. He decided to maintain a passive attitude, until either the Protectionists established themselves, or the party was reunited. Robert Peel died in 1850, but the Peelites remained opposed to reunion, and continued to function as a separate group.

In February 1851, the Radicals succeeded in carrying a motion in the Commons, favouring equalisation of the borough and county franchises. Although the Conservatives were opposed to equalisation, they did not support the government in the division, seeing a chance to bring it down. Russell resigned as Prime Minister, and Stanley tried to form a Conservative and Peelite coalition. The Peelites refused the suggestion, whereupon Stanley, advised by senior colleagues, decided against forming a government, feeling the Conservatives lacked potential ministerial ability – although Disraeli favoured this course. Russell, and the Whigs, returned to office. At the beginning of 1852, Disraeli became sole Leader of the Conservatives in the Commons. This followed the resignation of Granby from the triumvirate, on the grounds that it was not functioning, and its consequent collapse. Russell and the Whig government resigned again, in February 1852, after Lord Palmerston, recently dismissed from the post of Foreign Secretary, carried an amendment to their Militia Bill. Queen Victoria asked Stanley, who had become the Fourteenth Earl of Derby (in June of the previous year), to form a government. The prospects for the Conservatives were no better than a year earlier, but Derby decided to take office.

Having failed to gain outside support, Derby was forced to form a purely Conservative government, in which only three members had served under Peel. Disraeli became a minister for the first time, as Chancellor of the Exchequer. An Election was held in July, during which the Conservatives made it clear that they believed in the defence of the agricultural interest, but did not advocate a return to the Corn Laws. The Conservatives made gains at the Election, but were unable to secure a majority. The Whigs and the Radicals won 319 seats between them, the Conservatives 290, and the Peelites 45. In November, the Whigs brought a motion to the Commons, which acknowledged the triumph of free trade, and this was accepted by 468 votes to 53.

During December, the Peelites, led by William Gladstone, combined with the Whigs to defeat Disraeli's budget – which proposed to reduce the malt tax, to compensate the landed class for loss of the Corn Laws – and Derby resigned. The first Conservative government since the fall of Peel lasted less than a year, and achieved nothing of note.

Although a minority continued to cling to old hopes, most Conservatives accepted that a return to protection was not possible. They acted in response to political reality, rather than as a result of conversion. Various schemes for a reintroduction of protection, with preferential rates for parts of the British Empire, were destined to enthuse later generations of Conservative MPs, from 1903 onwards. One of these was put into law, by the Tory-dominated National Government, during 1932. Following this, protection remained an important part of British trading relations, despite adherence to the General Agreement on Tariffs and Trade (GATT), which sought to reduce tariffs across the world, from its commencement in 1948, during a period of Labour government. Free trade was dominant during Britain's membership of the European Economic Community / European Union, between 1973 and 2020. Despite protection being a major theme across a large spell of their party history, in recent times Conservatives have liked to give the impression of long-term support for free trade. There has been much talk of Global Britain, a concept introduced in 2016 by Theresa May and Boris Johnson (as Prime Minister and Foreign Secretary respectively), doing major post-Brexit deals with other leading economies, but success has been slow to materialise.

Back at the end of 1852, the Whigs and Peelites formed a coalition government, with the Peelite Earl of Aberdeen as Prime Minister. The Conservative Party organisation was in a dilapidated state so Disraeli set about rebuilding it. He appointed Sir William Jolliffe as Chief Whip, in place of Beresford. Jolliffe was entrusted with the overall management of the party, but the daily work of electoral management was carried out by Philip Rose, Disraeli's solicitor, who was appointed to the position of agent. Rose was assisted by Markham Spofforth, another partner in a London firm of solicitors – Baxter, Rose, Norton and Co. The appointments of Rose and Spofforth were significant as neither were MPs. Adversity had forced the party to adopt a more professional approach. Disraeli founded a party newspaper, *The Press*, with the first issue appearing in 1853, but this made little impact, and folded in 1866. Despite new developments, the whips remained significant figures in party organisation, and the Carlton Club, which moved to a new building in Pall Mall during 1854, was still a focal point.

Derby continued to follow a passive approach, partly because he did not believe that the Conservatives were capable of holding office, and partly due to ill health. Disraeli favoured active opposition, but was unable to make much impact. The government introduced a Reform Bill in 1854, only to withdraw it. Meanwhile they led Britain into the Crimea War, allying with Turkey and France against Russia. In January 1855, the Radicals carried a motion in the Commons to set up a committee to investigate the government's handling of the war – most of the Conservatives voted for the motion. Aberdeen resigned, and the queen invited Derby to form an administration. Having failed to obtain any outside support, Derby decided against attempting a purely Conservative government, believing it would fail, in a repeat of 1852.

3 The Truce of Parties

Lord Palmerston became Prime Minister in 1855, leading a coalition of Whigs and Peelites. The Conservatives admired Palmerston, and sympathised with the policies he followed, which showed him to be better placed to counter radicalism than they were. On the other hand, the Conservatives, hoping to return to power in their own right, were unwilling to receive the Peelites back. The Crimea war dragged on inconclusively until the start of 1856. Palmerston was defeated in the Commons, in March 1857, over his handling of the Chinese War. An Election followed the same month, at which the Whigs and Radicals won 372 seats, and a majority of 90. The Conservatives took 256 seats, while the Peelites were reduced to 26 MPs. In January 1858, Felice Orsini, an Italian revolutionary, attempted to assassinate Napoleon III of France. Orsini planned the attempt in Britain, and Napoleon protested to the government over the event. Palmerston introduced the Conspiracy Bill, aimed at preventing a repeat of the incident. The Conservatives attacked this, as subservience to a foreign power, the Bill was defeated, and Palmerston resigned.

Derby formed his second minority Conservative government, with Disraeli as Chancellor of the Exchequer. Although the Peelite group were not reconciled, General Peel, brother of Robert, joined the administration as Secretary for War. Lord Stanley, Derby's son, was Secretary for the Colonies. The government passed some useful legislation, including removal of the property qualification for Members of Parliament – not realising that it was illogical to require electors to be wealthier than those they elected. Besides this they admitted Jews to Parliament, despite Bentinck being driven from the leadership, a decade earlier, for supporting such a course. The government introduced a Reform Bill at the beginning of 1859, maintaining the borough franchise at £10, but reducing the county franchise to that level. The attempt to end the distinction between the county and borough franchises provoked the resignations of two

Cabinet ministers, Joseph Henley and Spencer Walpole. Derby believed equalisation would give the settlement the appearance of finality, allowing the powerful to unite against further Reform. The Bill included constituency redistribution, designed to strengthen the Conservatives' position. On March 31, the Whigs carried an amendment, on Second Reading in the Commons, by 39 votes, to lower the borough qualification,. Parliament was dissolved, and an Election held in May. The Conservatives made gains, but were again defeated, taking 306 seats against 348 for the combined forces of the Whigs, Radicals, and Peelites. On June 12, the opposition carried a Commons motion of no confidence, by 323 votes to 310, and Derby resigned, with his second government having proved little improvement upon the first.

Palmerston formed a government, and the non-Conservative groups in Parliament soon united, with the Liberal Party banner. This party was destined to merge with the Social Democratic Party, becoming the Social and Liberal Democrats in 1988, a name shortened to the Liberal Democrats during 1989. Although personally unenthusiastic, Palmerston allowed Russell to introduce a Reform Bill, in March 1860. The Bill differed little from that introduced by the Conservatives the previous year, but they decided to oppose it. The Bill received its Second Reading at the beginning of May. It was clear that the government was not wholly committed to the Bill, and that many Liberal MPs disliked it. Derby assured Palmerston that the Conservatives would not ally with potential Liberal rebels. This pledge influenced the government in withdrawing the Reform Bill, on June 11. That same day, Disraeli wrote to Sir William Miles, a leading backbencher, saying he had decided to resign as Leader, as the Conservative MPs were dissatisfied with him. After receiving Disraeli's letter, Miles consulted the leading members of the party in the Commons. The response was that the party did not want Disraeli to resign. Miles duly informed Disraeli, and persuaded him to remain as Leader.

Derby's health deteriorated, but there were not any moves to replace him as Leader, with the Conservatives uninterested in active opposition, or the pursuit of office. For several years, there was a tacit truce between the two political parties. Derby decided that the best course was to support Palmerston, against the radical section of the Liberals, and Palmerston was happy to govern with informal Conservative support. At this time, the Conservatives were acting from a position of weakness. In the future, the Conservatives would incorporate breakaway sections from the Liberals, during 1886 and 1947. Besides leading multi-party coalition governments in both World Wars, the Conservatives were destined to dominate a peacetime Coalition administration with the Liberal Party, from 1918 to 1922. Their Liberal Democrat successors would also be subordinate to the Conservatives, in a Coalition government, between 2010 and 2015, with David Cameron as Prime Minister.

Palmerston, and the moderate Liberals of his time, shared Tory veneration of traditional institutions. In supporting the monarchy, and House of Lords, the Conservative Party has done a disservice to the nation, promoting pre-democratic elements in our society. The Conservatives like to think the British are a particularly conservative nation. This belief ignores the enormous contribution of British people to the achievements of democracy, and the improved quality of human life. The Conservative Party has always held a pessimistic outlook, setting itself against the march of progress. As Conservatives have always needed to compromise with change, they cannot demonstrate having upheld any fixed principles. Whenever it defends the existing order of society at a particular point in time, Toryism is forced into defending aspects it formerly opposed.

In 1862, Alfred, a son of Queen Victoria, was offered the vacant role of king of Greece. Alfred declined, and the Greeks considered the alternative of Lord Stanley, as a British aristocrat, but this promotion from Conservative politician to monarch did not happen. The Greeks eventually chose a Danish prince, who became King George the following year. During

1864, Palmerston's government nearly involved Britain in the Schleswig-Holstein war, in which Prussia and Austria defeated Denmark. The Conservatives defeated the Liberals in the Lords on this issue, but the government won a vote in the Commons, and remained in office. The Liberals held a General Election in July 1865, winning 358 seats to the Conservatives' 300, thus increasing their majority. Derby had lost his fifth General Election out of five as Conservative Leader. He despaired of a return to power, but the political situation suddenly changed, as Palmerston died, on October 18. Disraeli privately concluded "the truce of parties is over", and anticipated "tempestuous times".

Earl Russell – as Lord John Russell had become in 1861 – was appointed Prime Minister, and the new government was led in the Commons by Gladstone. The latter introduced a Reform Bill, in March 1866, which proposed lowering the borough franchise to a £7 rental level, and the county franchise to a £14 rental level. These provisions would have harmed the Conservatives. In their campaign against the Reform Bill, the Conservatives were aided by the right wing of the Liberal Party, known as the Adullamites. The Bill received its Second Reading in April, but only by 318 votes to 313. On June 18, the Conservatives helped the Adullamites to carry an amendment in committee, which substituted a £7 rating level for the £7 rental level in the boroughs. This would have the effect of reducing the number of newly enfranchised electors. As it was clear the government would be unable to carry its Bill, Russell resigned on June 26.

4 A Leap in the Dark

Lord Derby formed his third minority Conservative government in June 1866. Once again, Disraeli was Chancellor of the Exchequer, while Lord Stanley was now elevated to be Foreign Secretary. Although the Conservatives were opposed to increasing the franchise, they saw that a Reform Bill could increase their public support. Disraeli put a plan to the Cabinet in February 1867, based on household suffrage in the boroughs. This provoked the resignation of three Cabinet ministers, Robert Gascoyne-Cecil (Viscount Cranbourne), Henry Herbert, Fourth Earl of Carnarvon, and General Peel. As these ministers rose to leave the Cabinet room, Derby remarked "This is the end of the Conservative Party". Unfortunately Derby proved to be wrong.

The Reform Bill was presented to the Commons in March. The borough franchise was based on household suffrage, but with a number of restrictions, while the county franchise was set at a £15 rating level. Passage of the Bill saw Disraeli directing operations, in brilliant style. The Bill received its Second Reading without a division. Thereafter, with the Conservatives being in a minority position, the Liberals were able to amendments, which removed the attempted restriction of borough household suffrage, and set the county franchise at £12. The Bill sought to exclude men in the boroughs who compounded – the term given to paying local rates via rent (rather than directly) – from the franchise. Grosvenor Hodgkinson, a backbench Liberal, proposed an amendment to abolish the compounding process, which would probably add several hundred thousand men to the electoral roll. Disraeli surprised the Commons by immediately accepting the Hodgkinson amendment – without even consulting any Cabinet colleagues – rather than getting held up with a debate, and contested vote, on the idea. Disraeli acted to retain the initiative, being focussed on the aim of the Tories, rather than the Liberals, carrying Reform.

The Bill received its Third Reading in the Commons in July. Derby proceeded to take the scheme through the Lords without difficulty. At the Third Reading, Derby admitted, on August 6, that the measure was "a leap in the dark". In private Derby responded to a friend, who argued that the Bill was dangerous, with the question "Don't you see how we have dished the Whigs?". The Conservatives had indeed outmanoeuvred their opponents. In doing so they had passed a Bill more radical than the one they defeated the previous year. The Reform Act was a major advance, but it still left Britain with a far from democratic franchise. The poorer section of the urban working class, the non-urban working class, and all women, remained excluded from the franchise. An attempt to extend the franchise to women was defeated, largely due to Conservative votes, in the Commons. The idea was proposed by John Stuart Mill, a political theorist who had a short spell as a Liberal MP. Mill famously introduced the idea of the Conservatives being "the stupid party", with their distrust of intellectualism.

The Conservatives were generally pleased with the Act, but it represented a defeat for them. They had been forced into carrying the Act by the necessity of the political situation, and were unable to protect ruling class dominance of the electorate. In the course of increasing their public support, the Conservatives attacked the social order they existed to defend. The Reform Act was followed by the formation of the National Union of Conservative and Constitutional Associations. The first meeting, held on November 12, at the Freemasons Tavern, in London, and chaired by John Gorst, a backbench MP, attracted representatives from more than 50 Conservative associations. This meeting was to be the first of a series of annual meetings of the National Union, which later became known as the Conservative Party Conference.

In February 1868, Derby was forced to retire on medical advice. After 22 years, Derby had finally resigned the Leadership of the Conservatives, and Disraeli became Prime Minister. Derby was replaced as Conservative Leader in the

Lords by Lord Malmesbury. The government carried Irish and Scottish Reform Acts in 1868, to complement the English legislation. Meanwhile the Corrupt Practices Act was the first major measure to deal with bribery at elections. Another Act allowed the Post Office to purchase the telegraph companies – the Conservatives carried out the first piece of nationalisation in Britain. Once the new register was complete, a General Election was held in November. The Conservatives did not conduct an effective campaign, and the National Union played virtually no role. The Conservatives won 279 seats, far behind the Liberals' 379 MPs. Disraeli resigned as Prime Minister upon the Election defeat, rather than waiting to be defeated by Parliament, breaking with existing practice.

A Liberal government was formed, with William Gladstone as Prime Minister. Malmesbury retired as the Conservative Leader in the House of Lords, being was replaced by Lord Cairns. On December 29, the second annual meeting of the National Union was held. Holding the meeting during the Christmas season did not prove to be a good idea, as it was attended by only seven members of the party. Cairns disliked being Leader of the Conservatives peers so he resigned at the end of 1869. In October, Lord Stanley became the Fifteenth Earl of Derby, on his father's death. The new Earl looked set to lead the party in the Lords, but declined the chance, and the Duke of Richmond took on the role. Disraeli still did not enjoy the full confidence of the Conservative Party. During 1871 and 1872 there were suggestions that he should resign as Leader, allowing Derby to take the post. Meanwhile the Liberals carried a major legislative programme, which the Conservatives were unable to block.

In 1870, Gerald Noel, the Conservative Chief Whip, offered the position of the party's leading agent to John Gorst, who was installed, on Disraeli's initiative, in a new office at Parliament Street, in Westminster. This soon came to be known as the Central Office, and in 1871 Gorst took the title of Principal Agent. During 1872, the headquarters of the National Union moved to the building occupied by Central Office. From that time onwards, the two organisations worked in conjunction, while the Carlton Club lost its political influence. Disraeli enhanced the status of the National Union in 1872, making it his audience for two major speeches, at the Free Trade Hall in Manchester, on May 3, and Crystal Palace in London, on June 24. The main theme was an attack on the Liberals, but Disraeli set out the principles of the Conservatives in the latter speech. Disraeli described the Conservatives as "a national party", with three main aims. These were, firstly "to maintain the institutions of the country", secondly "to uphold the Empire of England", and thirdly "the elevation of the condition of the people". The London speech has been revered by Conservatives, as among the most important pronouncements on their outlook, ever since 1872. It has failed to improve upon Disareli's words, in the following century and a half.

The Conservatives' claim to be a national party were merely a deception, prompted by a wish to appear to stand for something other than narrow self-interest, and thereby win support from the electorate. The Conservatives developed, from a party of the landed class, into the representative of those who held either land or capital, in opposition to the working class. Since passing the 1867 Reform Act, the Conservative Party has generally been electorally successful. The basis of this has been the hegemony of the ruling class, with the Conservatives acting to maintain that position. Power has given the Tories the opportunity to instil into the population a belief in the inevitability of Britain being a hierarchical society. The party has consistently failed to benefit the people of Britain, in return for being entrusted with their votes. It has perpetuated the existence of reactionary ideas. The Conservatives have always defended private property, as it is vital to their class power. They have sought to disguise this, by claiming that property allows people to be independent of the state. Conservative defence of capitalist property has maintained an economic system that exploits the labour of the majority, for the profit of a minority. The party's support for private property was also linked to their traditional argument against the existence of strong central authority. The Conservatives realised that such an authority could be used by their political opponents to attack the ruling class. There was a break with the usual Conservative practice during the 1980s, as the government of Margaret Thatcher, with an authoritarian outlook, significantly increased the power of the central government machinery, at the expense of local government, and other elements in the political structure of the nation. Conservative Prime Ministers since Thatcher have continued to support a centralised approach to the state. Power, and wealth, are both hereditary in the monarchy and aristocracy, leading to Conservatives supporting the institution of family life, while being a strong ally of the, very traditional, Church of England.

In March 1873, a Liberal rebellion led to the government's Irish University Bill being defeated. This in turn prompted the resignation of the government. Disraeli, however, declined to take office, believing that there was something to be gained by waiting. Gladstone failed to revive his government prior to the next Election, held in February 1874. The National Union played an important part in the campaign, helping the Conservatives win 352 seats, ahead of the Liberals on 243 seats, and the Irish Nationalists with 57 MPs. Gladstone resigned, and Disraeli became Prime Minister. The Conservative Party's "leap in the dark" had belatedly proved successful. Seven years after the passage of the second Reform Act, they had been returned to power with a clear majority. Richmond led the government in the Lords, while Derby was Foreign Secretary. Disraeli was able to secure the inclusion of the Third Marquess of Salisbury – as Robert Gascoyne-Cecil had become – and the Earl of Carnarvon.

This government was destined to enter into party mythology as an example of what could be achieved by a Conservative administration. In the process the term Disraelianism was to enter their vocabulary, as a major tradition in the party, which has been as influential as Peelism. It is characteristic of the faulty reasoning of Conservatives that the Disraelian tradition is based on very slight foundations. While Disraeli lived there was no conscious policy of Disraelianism. The approach Disraeli is credited with was developed by Conservative Party thinkers after he died. It was also a very selective interpretation. Various fragments from the diverse career of Disraeli have been taken to represent a coherent approach, while details which do not fit the picture have been silently disregarded. Disraeli is held to have followed a policy that went by the name of "One Nation". The essential features of this are the promotion of national unity, with patriotism, and a progressive domestic policy, aimed at avoiding class conflict. The reality is far less impressive. Disraeli did not use the words "One Nation" to describe his policy, but had described the division between rich and poor, in the novel *Sybil, or, the Two Nations*. The phrase "One Nation" was not to be introduced until 1950, when a group of MPs formed an informal discussion circle, aimed at advancing progressive Conservative views. They looked to Disraeli as their mentor, and called themselves the One Nation Group, by adapting the title of the novel. From this a legend emerged that Disraeli had coined the phrase "One Nation". During 2019, a new One Nation Conservatives group was set up, attempting to direct an echo of Disraeli against advocates of a hard-line Brexit, but without success.

Ever since Disraeli was their Leader, the Conservatives have proclaimed themselves to be patriotic. In practice the Conservatives have been the party of nationalism, seeking a powerful position in the world for Britain at the expense of other countries. The Conservative Party has also been an English rather than a British Party. Its electoral support has always been stronger in England than the state as a whole. Besides lacking a name for his policy, Disraeli did not really have a programme. The Conservative Party has revered Disraeli for possession of an ideology which he did not hold. Celebration of the imaginary theories of Peelism and Disraelianism contrasts with the party's pride in a non-ideological approach. This paradox reflects the incoherence of much Conservative Party's thinking.

In 1874, Disraeli did not have a plan for his government to implement, but some social reform was carried the following year. At the end of 1875, Disraeli organised the government's purchase of Khedive Ismail's shares in the Suez Canal Company, giving Britain control of a major trading route, that led to India. Disraeli carried the Royal Titles Act 1876, which secured the designation Empress of India for Queen Victoria. The government's social reform programme dwindled, as it became preoccupied with foreign affairs. Disraeli was created the Earl of Beaconsfield, in August 1876, and moved to the House of Lords. Disraeli installed Stafford Northcote, the Chancellor of the Exchequer, as the Leader of the Conservatives in the Commons.

Disraeli found himself confronted with the Eastern Question. The three Powers of the Dreikaiserbund – Germany, Russia, and Austria – had recently sought to press reforms on Turkey. Disraeli felt that Britain had a legitimate interest in the fate of Turkey. Months of negotiations, and sporadic fighting, were the result, with Britain taking the side of Turkey against Russia. Derby and Carnarvon resigned from the government in protest at Disraeli involving Britain in war. Salisbury replaced Derby as Foreign Secretary, and managed to arrange peace. A full settlement was agreed at the Congress of Berlin, during June and July 1878. Disraeli proved to be the outstanding figure at the Congress, and returned home in triumph, announcing he had secured "peace with honour".

Britain faced a serious agricultural depression. Having brought down Peel over the issue, Disraeli seemed ideally placed to reintroduce protection, but declared the question had been settled. Disraeli accepted that agriculture had ceased to dominate the British economy. As the government's term in office progressed, it increasingly lost its way, and suffered two imperial debacles. The first stemmed from an attempt to federate the provinces of South Africa, which led to war with the Zulus.

On January 22 1879, Zulus massacred the forces defending the British camp at Isandhlwana. Although war ended in British victory in July, the government was unable to overcome the political damage of the initial disaster. An attempt to conquer Afghanistan was thwarted, as Afghan soldiers massacred the staff of the British Legation, at Kabul, on September 3.

A previous Anglo-Afghan War had ended with defeat for Britain, back in 1842, when Robert Peel had been the Conservative Prime Minister. A century after British intervention under Disraeli, the Soviet Union invaded Afghanistan during 1979, in support of a government that was facing rebellion. This action was condemned by Margaret Thatcher, who had recently taken power, upon a Conservative General Election victory. Thatcher authorised a covert British role in Afghanistan, during the 1980s, supporting the Mujahideen rebels. This sowed the seeds of later disaster, with Osama bin Laden, one of the Mujahideen leaders, forming Al-Qaeda, whose terrorists attacked the USA, on September 11 2001. This in turn led to the USA, with support from Britain, invading Afghanistan, to remove the Taliban, allies of Al-Qaeda, from power, setting off another twenty years of war.

In March 1880, the Disraeli government called a General Election for the following month. At the same time, they hurried through a Parliamentary Elections and Corrupt Practices Act. Instead of tackling corruption, this law was mainly designed to help the Conservative Party (wealthier than the Liberals), by allowing candidates to pay money for the transport of electors to the polls, in borough constituencies. The Conservatives failed to make much use of the National Union in the Election campaign. The party organisation had declined, following the end of Gorst's tenure as Principal Agent in 1874, and the Conservative leadership were not prepared to concede influence to ordinary members. It was not until 1876 that the Party Conference was permitted to pass resolutions, but it was barred from discussing policy issues. The deference of the membership – with reverence for hierarchy – ensured that the resolutions passed over the next few years were limited to meaningless expressions of support for the leadership. The Liberals won 352 seats in the General Election, and a majority of 52, ahead of the Conservatives with 237 MPs, and the Irish Nationalists on 63. Disraeli resigned, and Gladstone became Prime Minister of a Liberal government.

Benjamin Disraeli died a year after leaving office, on April 19 1881, at the age of 76. The Conservative Party lost its greatest ever figure. Disraeli had limitations, most notably a failure to embrace democracy, but the Conservatives have never found his equal. The Conservatives have failed to appreciate the true value of Disraeli, revering him as the founder of Disraelianism, which never actually existed. Disraeli's real strength lay in his being an adventurer, and a politician with imagination, in contrast to the stale negativity of his party.

5 Bob's Your Uncle

The Conservative Party decided against choosing a single Leader upon the death of Disraeli. Salisbury was elected their Leader by the Conservative peers, while Northcote was re-elected by the MPs. In response to the 1880 General Election defeat, Disraeli had set up a committee, aimed at improving the party organisation. This was chaired by William Henry Smith, an MP who had been a member of Disraeli's recent government – he was also a leading figure in the W H Smith retail chain. Earl Percy, Chairman of the National Union, sat on the committee, as did John Gorst, now recalled to the Principal Agent role. The Party Conference agreed new rules in 1880, which resulted in the Council of the National Union being selected on a more representative basis. This was a victory for the middle class leaders of the constituency associations, who wished to secure more influence for themselves.

The "Fourth Party" emerged as a set of rebellious Conservative MPs, intent on undermining Northcote, who was a weak Leader. The group was comprised of Lord Randolph Churchill, John Gorst, Arthur Balfour – a nephew of Salisbury – and Sir Henry Drummond Wolff. Churchill, the effective leader of the Fourth Party, had a political outlook even more confused than was generally the case in the Conservative Party. Part of the reason for Churchill's increasingly erratic behaviour was the onset of a brain disease, which eventually led to his death, in 1895. Speaking in Parliament, during November 1882, he referred to "the great Tory democracy, which Lord Beaconsfield partly constructed, that was formed in 1874". This led to some enthusiasm, during the next few years, for the idea of Tory democracy. In the longer term, Churchill has been lauded by Conservatives, as the leading advocate for this element in the party's development, and a worthy successor to Disraeli. Tory Democracy is actually a myth, built on foundations that shift as much as the One Nation idea, attributed to Disraeli decades after his death. Tory Democracy was spoken of by Churchill, but on very few occasions. At the time of the 1885 General Election, he privately defined the outlook as being "principally opportunism", while publicly saying "The Tory democracy is a democracy which has embraced the principles of the Tory party". Randolph Churchill merely had a phrase, and lacked a programme.

Gorst's role in the "Fourth Party" put him in an anomalous position, given that he was a member of the party committee, which was responsible to the leadership. Nevertheless, with Northcote not feeling able to move against him, Gorst remained a member of the committee, until November 1882, when he resigned following a quarrel with the whips. In April 1883, the Fourth Party founded the Primrose League, in honour of Disraeli – primroses having reputedly been his favourite flower. The League was not an official organ of the Conservative Party, but it was directed by members of the party, and worked in the interests of the Conservatives. Membership of the Primrose League bloomed, partly because it was open to women, despite the Tories being opposed to giving them the vote. This outlook only changed when a Liberal-led Coalition government, recognising the role of women in World War One, extended the franchise in 1918. Thereafter the Primrose League wilted, and it was disbanded in 2004.

Churchill began to see himself as a possible Leader, and latched on to the demands of the National Union. He and Gorst aimed to secure control of party policy, and an increased role in the party organisation, for the National Union. Churchill's campaign led to the resignation of Lord Percy as Chairman of the National Union, in February 1884, following which Churchill took the role. In May, Churchill staged a tactical resignation as Chairman of the National Union. He was re-elected a fortnight after his resignation, thereby further increasing his standing. The Fourth Party's attack on Northcote allowed Salisbury to assert himself as the dominant partner in the joint Leadership. He negotiated with Churchill, to end the struggle in the party, and agreement was reached in June 1884.

Salisbury was opposed to any increase in the power of the National Union. Churchill now came to share this view, realising that a strengthened National Union might threaten his own position if he became Leader. The party committee was disbanded, having been inefficient, and its responsibilities reverted to Salisbury. Churchill handed over the chairmanship of the National Union to Sir Michael Hicks Beach. In 1885, the Party Conference was finally allowed to pass policy resolutions – eighteen years after the Nation Union was founded. Salisbury appointed Richard Middleton as Principal Agent. An ex-naval officer, erroneously known to the Conservatives as Captain Middleton, he would hold the role from 1885 to 1903 – a spell of eighteen years – and ensure the party organisation was more effectively managed.

The Liberal Government introduced a Reform Bill, to equalise the franchise. Randolph Churchill displayed the shallowness of his commitment to democracy, by opposing the Bill. It was not clear what Tory Democracy meant, but it was clear that it did not include extension of the franchise. The Reform Bill passed through the Commons without difficulty, but was held up in the Lords. Conservative peers pressed for a Redistribution Bill, hoping to confuse matters. Gladstone refused to allow the Lords to block the Bill so Salisbury, seeing that defiance by the Lords would play into the hands of the Liberals, reached a settlement with Gladstone. The Reform Bill and a Redistribution Bill were passed as agreed measures, the first in 1884, and the second in 1885. The Conservatives gained the support of the Irish Nationalists, by offering to end coercion, and the two parties united to carry an amendment to the budget on June 8 1885. Gladstone resigned the following day.

Lord Salisbury became Prime Minister, and was elected the overall Leader of the Conservative Party. Salisbury also took on the post of Foreign Secretary, feeling himself to be the best person for the task. Churchill joined the government, as Indian Secretary, on condition that Northcote be replaced as the Leader of the party in the Commons. Salisbury reluctantly gave

Northcote a peerage, creating him Earl of Iddesleigh, and appointed Sir Michael Hicks Beach as Leader of the House of Commons. Churchill soon wished to resign, following a disagreement with Salisbury over Indian policy, but the latter persuaded him to remain in his post. With the new register complete, Salisbury held a General Election, in November. The Liberals won 334 seats, the Conservatives 250, and the Irish Nationalists 86. Gladstone now declared himself to be in favour of Home Rule for Ireland. The Irish Nationalists allied with the Liberals, and they combined, in January 1886, to defeat the government in the Commons, on an English agricultural issue, prompting Salisbury to resign.

Salisbury was succeeded by Gladstone and the Liberals. Gladstone introduced a Home Rule Bill in April, offering Ireland self-government, but not independence. The Conservatives attacked the Bill, conveniently forgetting their recent opportunistic alliance with the Irish Nationalists. Churchill led the way with the far from democratic phrase "Ulster will fight and Ulster will be right". This was a reference to the opposition to Home Rule from the Protestant section of the Irish population, concentrated in Ulster. The Conservatives portrayed opposition to Home Rule as a constitutional matter, but their attachment to the Union was also rooted in the British landed class possessing vast estates in Ireland. The radicals in the Liberal Party favoured Home Rule, while the aristocratic section, led by Lord Hartington, opposed it. The Home Rule Bill was defeated on the Second Reading, in the Commons, during June 1886, by 343 votes to 313, with 93 Liberals voting against it. Gladstone called an Election for July, during which the Conservatives and Liberal Unionists, as they became known, fought as an alliance. The Conservatives emerged as the largest party with 316 seats, while the Liberal Unionists won 78. The Liberal Party was reduced to 191 seats, and the Irish Nationalists won 85 seats. The combined forces of the Conservatives and the Liberal Unionists had won 394 seats, with Churchill giving the name Unionists to this alliance. Gladstone resigned upon the Liberals' defeat, and the queen summoned Salisbury.

Before visiting the queen, Salisbury asked Hartington to take the premiership in a coalition government, but the latter felt unable to commit himself to the Conservative Party. Salisbury thus formed his second minority Conservative administration. Salisbury chose not to take on the burden of being Foreign Secretary, giving this role to Iddesleigh. Hicks Beach was replaced as Leader of the House of Commons by Churchill, who was also Chancellor of the Exchequer. Arthur Balfour, Secretary for Scotland, entered the Cabinet in November. The Autumn saw a Cabinet dispute over the budget. Churchill proposed a major restructuring of the taxation system, linked with spending on social projects, partly financed by a reduction in expenditure on the armed services. The Cabinet – particularly the Secretary for War, W H Smith – were opposed, and Churchill resigned in December. Whereas Churchill bounced back after a tactical resignation as Chairman of the National Union in 1884, and asserted his position with the threat to resign as Indian Secretary in 1885, he was not able to carry out another successful challenge. Churchill overlooked the fact that the public were unable to judge his case, as the budget discussions were secret. Salisbury reconstructed his government during January 1887. First he made another attempt to persuade Hartington to take on the premiership, but this failed. On the other hand, a Liberal Unionist, Viscount Goschen, agreed to become Chancellor of the Exchequer. Salisbury became Foreign Secretary, as Iddesleigh resigned due to ill health – he died within days. W H Smith was Leader of the House of Commons. When Hicks Beech retired, a few weeks later, he was replaced as Irish Secretary by Balfour. Robert Cecil's nepotism in advancing the career of Balfour, his nephew, led to the coining of the phrase "Bob's Your Uncle".

Salisbury was an intellectual, but lacked respect for new ideas, preferring to find ways to defend a reactionary outlook. He wished to follow a negative line, merely obstructing progress, but showed some positive intentions, to retain Liberal Unionist support, and remain safely in power. The Local Government Act of 1888 was their main achievement, creating County Councils for England and Wales. In October 1891, W H Smith died, and Salisbury appointed Balfour as Leader of the House of Commons. In December, Hartington's father died so he went to the Lords, as the Duke of Devonshire, and Joseph Chamberlain became Leader of the Liberal Unionists in the Commons. In July 1892, Salisbury held a General Election, with the Conservatives winning 268 seats, and the Liberal Unionists 47. The Liberals won 273 seats, and the Irish Nationalists 81. At the same time Keir Hardie was elected as an independent Socialist. The combined strength of the Conservatives and Liberal Unionists was 315 against 354 for the Liberals and Irish Nationalists. Salisbury chose to ignore the democratic precedents of Disraeli and Gladstone. Although he lost the Election, Salisbury did not resign until the Liberals carried a motion of no confidence, in the Commons, during August.

Gladstone formed a minority Liberal government and, in February 1893, introduced his second Home Rule Bill. The Bill faced resolute opposition, from the Conservatives and Liberal Unionists. It was finally passed by the Commons, in September, only to be defeated on Second Reading in the Lords. Gladstone's government was unable to achieve much as the Conservatives and Liberal Unionists used their majority in the Lords to block most of its legislation. The Conservatives justified their actions on the grounds that the Liberals lacked a majority, and were only maintained in office by the Irish Nationalists. The Tories conveniently forgot their recent minority government being bolstered, for six years, by the Liberal Unionists. Gladstone retired in March 1894, and was succeeded by Lord Rosebery. The Liberal Unionists made it clear to Salisbury that they would be willing to form a coalition government with the Conservatives, upon the fall from power of the Liberals. In June 1895 Henry Campbell-Bannerman, the Secretary for War, was censured by the Commons, for not having provided the army with enough cordite, and the government responded by resigning.

Salisbury became Prime Minister for the third time, leading a coalition of Conservatives and Liberal Unionists. The two parties forming the alliance became known as the Unionist Party. Salisbury was again Foreign Secretary as well as Prime Minister, and Arthur Balfour was Leader of the House of Commons. Having formed the government, Salisbury sought a majority at a General Election, held in July. The Unionists won 411 seats – the Conservatives 341 and the Liberal Unionists 70 – while the Liberal Party won 177 seats, and the Irish Nationalists 82. The government had a majority of 152 seats, and the only barrier to it carrying a programme was the absence of any concrete plan. The government produced little social legislation of note, on account of its lack of enthusiasm in this field, and its preoccupation with foreign affairs. The administration pledged to introduce old age pensions, but then decided against acting, on the grounds of the costs involved.

The Conservative and Liberal Unionist organisations remained separate, being based on different principles. The Conservative Party was hierarchical and dominated by the leadership, while the Liberal Unionist organisation was democratic. Salisbury provided a large proportion of the party's central finances, from the Cecil family fortune. The other major source of funding was a system of corruption, namely the sale of honours. In return for large donations to the party, prominent men were rewarded with titles by the government. The Conservative Party, formed to defend the exclusive position of the aristocracy, were now selling membership of that order to the highest bidders. It was a remarkable compromise of the party's principles. In selling peerages to capitalists, the Conservatives offered them an increase in status, to match their wealth, and also united them with the established landowning element of the ruling class.

Recent years have seen a revival of the Tory tradition of allocating places in the House of Lords to donors. The three

Prime Ministers in office since 2010 – David Cameron, Theresa May, and Boris Johnson – have each indulged in the practice. Perhaps the most notorious example has featured Peter Cruddas, a billionaire financier, who had a short spell as Co-Treasurer of the Conservatives, during 2011 and 2012. Cruddas resigned, amidst suggestions that he was planning a scheme of privileged access to Cameron, in return for cash from his fellow large-scale donors. Cruddas continued to make large donations to the party, and also gave financial support to Boris Johnson's successful Leadership campaign, in 2019. The following year, Johnson nominated his backer for a peerage, a recommendation that the House of Lords Appointments Commission refused to support, citing the 2012 allegations. Johnson over-ruled the commission, Lord Cruddas arrived in Parliament at the start of 2021 and, within a few days, made a new donation of £500,000 to the Tories.

The late nineteenth century struggle among European empires for land, and resources, across Africa was of particular interest to the Unionists. Rhodesia was established in 1895, with its capital Salisbury named after the Prime Minister. Britain conquered Sudan, following the Battle of Omdurman in 1898, and asserted its position in relation to France, in the Fashoda incident that year. In October 1899, the Boer War broke out in South Africa, as the British and Dutch populations each sought dominance of the territory. Although he attempted to prevent the outbreak of hostilities, Joseph Chamberlain, the Colonial Secretary, enthusiastically committed the British army to the war, rather than leaving the British colonists in South Africa to fight alone. The Boers were successful in the opening exchanges of the war, and by the end of 1899 clearly had the upper hand. During 1900, the British retrieved the situation, and then went on the offensive. Chamberlain believed that the government could benefit electorally, and persuaded Salisbury to call a General Election. At the "Khaki Election", held in October 1900, the Unionists took 408 seats – the Conservatives winning 334, and the Liberal Unionists 68 – while the Liberal Party won

184 seats, the Irish Nationalists 82, and the Labour Representation Committee 2.

Salisbury reconstructed the government, and lightened his personal burden by appointing Lord Lansdowne as Foreign Secretary. Arthur Balfour continued to lead the government in the Commons, while his brother Gerald entered the Cabinet as President of the Board of Trade. A fourth member of the family joined the Cabinet, as Salisbury's son-in-law, Lord Selbourne, became First Lord of the Admiralty. At the same time Lord Cranbourne, Salisbury's son, entered the government as Under Secretary at the Foreign Office. The government was referred to as the Hotel Cecil, a reference to a London hotel which the family owned. Arthur Balfour, clearly recognised as Salisbury's successor, acquired the nickname Prince Arthur. The Unionist Party seemed to be turning itself into a monarchy. The government was unable to take advantage of its electoral victory, as it was lacking in new ideas, while Salisbury's health failed rapidly. Queen Victoria died in January 1901, and was succeeded by Edward VII. The Boer War dragged on, without real progress for Britain, until the Peace of Vereeniging, in May 1902. Salisbury retired on July 11 – he died in August 1903.

Salisbury was duly succeeded as Prime Minister by Arthur Balfour, who was elected Unionist Leader on July 14. The Unionists showed a lack of constitutional propriety, holding their party meeting at the Foreign Office. Balfour's outlook followed that of Lord Salisbury, but he was a less able politician. Lord Lansdowne, a Liberal Unionist, replaced Salisbury as Unionist Leader in the Lords. Austen Chamberlain, son of Joseph, entered the Cabinet as Postmaster General. Balfour soon faced a controversy, which was to split his government. Joseph Chamberlain pressed for the introduction of Tariff Reform, whereby taxes would be introduced on imports, but with a preferential rate for goods from the British Empire. Chamberlain believed Imperial Preference was the way to retain the unity, and strength, of the Empire. He also hoped that revenue, from the duties, would be a source of finance for social reform. The Chancellor of the Exchequer, C T Ritchie, was opposed to this plan. The Cabinet discussed Chamberlain's scheme over a number of months, but no final decision was taken. In May 1903, Chamberlain publicly outlined his plans. This prompted protectionists in the Unionist Party to form the Tariff Reform League. In September, Chamberlain decided to resign, to be free to continue his attempt to win over the party. Balfour dismissed four free traders from the Cabinet, including Ritchie, for intriguing against him. Following this, the Duke of Devonshire, also a free trader, resigned.

The tariff plan lost the Unionist Party public support, as the new taxes would increase food prices. Some free traders stayed loyal to Balfour, in the hope of maintaining party unity, but others moved over to the Liberals. Winston Churchill, an MP who was the son of Randolph Churchill, joined the Liberals in 1904. Chamberlain and the tariff reformers gained control of the National Union. Balfour resigned as Prime Minister, on December 4 1905, but not as the result of any Parliamentary defeat. He hoped the Liberals would damage themselves, by returning to office as a minority government. Balfour's action was an admission of failure. After a decade in power, during which they achieved little, the Unionists had nothing else to offer.

6 Criminal Classes

The Liberals accepted the challenge laid down by Balfour, and took office at the end of 1905, with Henry Campbell-Bannerman as Prime Minister. The latter outmanoeuvred the former by calling an immediate General Election, held in January 1906. The Conservatives suffered their worst ever electoral defeat. The combined forces of the Unionist Party took a mere 157 seats – with 132 Conservative MPs and 25 Liberal Unionists. The Liberals won 401 seats, the Irish Nationalists 83, and Labour 29. The Liberal majority was 132. Balfour, who lost his seat at Manchester, announced it was necessary that "the great Unionist Party should still control, whether in power or whether in opposition, the destinies of this great empire". This absurd claim was not an isolated aberration on Balfour's part. It was merely the opening of a remarkable campaign by the Unionist Party against the Liberal government. The Unionists believed they had a right to determine how the country was governed, even although they had been rejected by the electorate. They remained the party of the ruling class, and determined to defend their interests. Balfour returned to the Commons, as MP for the City of London, at a By-Election, in March. In July, Joseph Chamberlain suffered a stroke, which forced him to retire. This reduced the effectiveness of the tariff reformers, but they still managed to dominate the party, as the free trade element declined in influence. The tariff reformers were dissatisfied with Balfour, who showed a lack of commitment to their cause. Balfour's main concern was the attack on the Liberal Government. He ensured that the Unionists continually delayed legislation in the Commons, and defeated it in the Lords. Balfour regarded the Unionist Party as one of the great institutions of the state, and believed that its function was to defend other such institutions. Illness forced Campbell-Bannerman to resign, in April 1908, and Herbert Asquith became Prime Minister. In 1909, David Lloyd George, the Chancellor of the Exchequer, introduced a budget that aimed to finance the government's social policy from taxation upon those most able to bear it. The Unionists came to the strange conclusion that the budget was unconstitutional, as it attacked the propertied class, and therefore deserved to be defeated. The Finance Bill was passed by the Commons on November 4. On November 30, the Unionists used their majority in the Lords to defeat the Bill's Second Reading. The government now secured a dissolution.

The Election was held in January 1910, with the Unionists winning 273 seats – 242 for the Conservatives and 31 for the Liberal Unionists – equal with 273 seats for the Liberal Party. The Irish Nationalists won 82 seats, and the Labour Party 40. The Liberal government was now reliant upon the Irish Nationalists. It planned to pass the budget, end the Lords' veto, and carry Home Rule. The Unionists argued that the Irish Nationalists were keeping the Liberals in office to bring about a constitutional revolution, for which there was no mandate. In view of this, the Unionists decided that a policy of extreme opposition was justified. The government drew up a Parliament Bill, proposing that any legislation passed by the House of Commons in three separate sessions would be exempt from the Lords' veto, and thus become law. The Bill was introduced in April, following which the Commons passed the budget, and the Lords then did likewise without a division – the Unionists deciding to concentrate on the attack on the Parliament Bill. In May, Edward VII died, delaying the expected confrontation, and offering the possibility of a negotiated settlement, in the cause of national unity. In June, a conference between the parties was set up, to discuss the issue of the House of Lords. The conference failed to find a solution, and broke up in November. Asquith called another Election, which was held in December, but left the state of the parties virtually unchanged. The Unionists with 272 seats – Conservatives 238 and Liberal Unionists 34 – were tied with the Liberal Party on 272 seats. The Irish Nationalists won 84 seats, and the Labour Party 42.

The Unionists' failure to make progress at the Election led to an internal enquiry. A Unionist Organisation Committee, formed in February 1911, representing all sections of the party, recommended the establishment of two new posts, those of Party Treasurer and Chairman of the Party. The latter would oversee the Central Office and the party in the country. The post of Chairman went to the backbencher Arthur Steel-Maitland, while Lord Farquhar became Party Treasurer. The government reintroduced the Parliament Bill in February, and it was passed by the Commons in May. The Bill then went through the Lords, being heavily amended. The government informed Balfour and Lord Lansdowne that George V had pledged to create peers, if this was necessary to carry the Bill. The Shadow Cabinet therefore decided to accept the Bill. Balfour left for a holiday, in Germany, before the Lords voted on the Third Reading. Lansdowne persuaded most Unionist peers to abstain in the vote, on August 10. Nevertheless 114 Unionists voted against the Bill, while 37 Unionists actually voted for it. It was only the Unionist votes for the Bill that allowed it to pass, by 131 votes to 114. Fundamentalists now considered forming a new party, feeling Balfour had betrayed them. They decided, however, that better hope lay in capturing the Unionist Party. They planned to launch an attack at the Party Conference, in November. Balfour was still in Germany, unaware of the campaign against him, but considering resignation. Upon his return, in September, Balfour learned of the attacks, and this strengthened his wish to step down. Balfour clearly no longer controlled the party and, at the beginning of November, he resigned..

The Conservatives had never previously experienced a contested Leadership election. Now there were two candidates, Austen Chamberlain and Walter Long, the latter being a fundamentalist. Chamberlain and Long agreed that they would each withdraw, should a strong third candidate emerge, as a contest would harm the party. Andrew Bonar Law now entered the contest, prompting both Chamberlain and Long to withdraw. The meeting to choose the Leader was held on November 13, at the Carlton Club, and Law was elected unanimously. Law, who had more respect for democracy than previous Conservative Leaders, took the role as the result of an election, albeit one in which he was ultimately unopposed. Law was an unlikely Leader of the Unionist Party. He had been born in Canada, into a family with an Ulster and Scottish background, and lacked his party's traditional feeling for the countryside and country houses. Law suffered a great deal from doubt, but managed to rouse himself to determined action, in the interests of the party he led. He was determined to secure the exclusion of Ulster from Home Rule, and also to retain Tariff Reform as a Unionist policy. While most members of the Unionist Party were opposed to Home Rule outright, Law was prepared to accept if Ulster was excluded. Law differed from his party in that he had sympathy for the claims of the working class. Law also favoured enfranchisement of women, but did not declare himself in public so as to avoid alienating his party. Women had begun to be accepted as members of the party over the previous few years, although they were restricted to a minor role. Officially the Unionist Party did not have view on the question of female suffrage. In practice most of its members were opposed, and the party acted against the enfranchisement of women. Law secured the merger of the Conservative and Liberal Unionist organisations, in 1912. The organisation was renamed the National Unionist Association of Conservative and Unionist Associations. The word Liberal was thus dropped while Conservative was retained.

In April 1912, the government introduced its Home Rule Bill. This offered Ireland self-government rather than independence, but the Unionists argued the Bill presented a fundamental constitutional issue, making illegal action justified. The Ulster Unionists, led by Edward Carson, set up a terrorist organisation, the Ulster Volunteers, and committed themselves to forming a provisional government, once the Bill passed. The Bill received its Second Reading in the Commons in May. On July 29, Law attended a Unionist demonstration against Home Rule at

Blenheim Palace, and made a speech about the possibility that Ulster would be forced to submit to a Parliament at Dublin. Law said "if such an attempt is made, I can imagine no length of resistance to which Ulster can go in which I should not be prepared to support them". Law demonstrated a willingness to resist the democratic process where he felt the issue demanded it. He suggested that the king might dismiss the government, rather than give Royal Assent, should Home Rule be passed, but the king declined this autocratic suggestion. Law pessimistically foresaw civil war as the result of his party's resistance to the government, but remained opposed to compromise over Ulster. Asquith considered taking legal action against leading Unionists for sedition, while exempting Law, as Leader of the Opposition, from this. Realising he anomaly of not acting against Law, Asquith dropped the idea.

The Home Rule Bill was passed by the Commons in early 1913, only to be rejected by the Lords. The Ulster Volunteers militia was now reorganised as the Ulster Volunteer Force (UVF). A new session of Parliament began in March, and the Home Rule Bill was again passed by the Commons, but rejected by the Lords in July. During the latter part of 1913, Law suggested to the king that he should dismiss the government, forcing an Election, to allow Home Rule to be put to the electorate, but George V opposed this idea. The Liberals and the Unionists began to look for a compromise, on the basis of excluding Ulster, but no agreement was reached. The Ulster Unionists carried out military, and political, preparations to set up a provisional government. They seemed fully competent to do so, with the result that the Liberal government would have to use the army if it was to enforce Home Rule. In February 1914, Law suggested to the Shadow Cabinet that the party use the House of Lords to amend the annual Army Bill. The amendment would decree that the army could not be used in Ulster until after a General Election. In the event that the amendment was carried, the government would be forced to dissolve Parliament. If the amendment was rejected, the Unionists planned to defeat the Bill, thus ending all military discipline in both Britain and Ireland. Either way the government would have to call an Election. In contemplating defeat of the Army Bill, the Unionists displayed a lack of the patriotism on which they prided themselves. The Unionists were prepared to deprive Britain of its army, at a time when Europe was threatened with war.

The government reintroduced the Home Rule Bill, in March, at the same time offering concessions to Ulster, which did not satisfy the Unionists. That month, army officers, stationed at the Curragh, carried out a mutiny, making it clear that they were not prepared to coerce Ulster. As a result, the Unionists did not feel they needed their plan to amend the Army Act. In April, the Unionists bought a large supply of arms in Germany, and smuggled them into Ulster for use by the UVF, preparing for civil war, an event known as the Larne gun-running. The Unionists then attacked the Liberals, with a censure motion in the Commons, claiming that the government was planning to seize control of Ulster. In the debate Winston Churchill, the former Unionist, remarked that the motion resembled "a vote of censure by the criminal classes upon the police". A century later, the Tories would unite with the political representatives of a subsequent version of the UVF, in the form of the misnamed Democratic Unionist Party. Theresa May's Conservative government lost its Parliamentary majority in 2017, but remained in power with DUP support for two more years.

The Home Rule Bill received its Third Reading, in the Commons, during May. Asquith, who feared the outbreak of a European war, and knew he could not coerce Ulster, arranged the Buckingham Palace Conference, with the Unionists, in July, but it failed to find a solution to the Home Rule question. At this point, international developments took over. The Home Rule struggle had nearly led to civil war, but this was averted by the outbreak of what became World War One. The Unionists were therefore rescued from the consequences of their rash actions.

War against Germany was declared on August 4. The Home Rule Act was passed, through use of the Parliament Act, soon after the outbreak of war, along with an Act suspending it until after the war. A party truce was agreed, ending contested By-Elections, and the next General Election, due by the end of 1915, was postponed. The Unionist Party was in a difficult position, feeling hostile to the government, but having to restrain itself in the national interest. In May 1915, the First Sea Lord, John Fisher, resigned as a result of disagreement with the government over naval strategy, for which Churchill was responsible as First Lord of the Admiralty. This was a crisis, and Law informed the government that he was not able to contain his party any longer. Law pressed that a coalition was necessary, and Asquith accepted this.

Asquith retained the premiership in the Coalition government, while Law was Colonial Secretary. Lansdowne took a place in the Cabinet as Minister without Portfolio, besides continuing to lead the Unionist Party in the Lords. Balfour became First Lord of the Admiralty, replacing Churchill, who was moved to the post of Chancellor of the Duchy of Lancaster. Formation of the Coalition led to some improvement in the conduct of the war, but the military situation remained deadlocked. The Unionists were divided over whether they should continue to support Asquith, and there was a movement of opinion in favour of Lloyd George among the Liberals.

In December 1916, Law and Lloyd George persuaded Asquith to resign. Lloyd George became Prime Minister, and put control of the government into the hands of a small War Cabinet, with Law as Chancellor of the Exchequer. Lord Curzon assumed the Leadership of the Unionists in the Lords, while Lansdowne left the government, as he was opposed to continuance of the war. Asquith went into opposition, leading dissident Liberals. Once Lloyd George became Prime Minister, the Unionists were generally satisfied with the government's handling of the war. With the United States of America joining the war, in April

1917, the tide turned in favour of Britain and her allies, against Germany and the other Central Powers.

The Coalition government carried a Representation of the People Act, in February 1918, which introduced full manhood suffrage, and gave the vote to women over the age of 30 who owned property. The Unionists managed to retain most of the existing plural votes, as these benefitted the party. The Unionist Party organisation, having worked at reduced capacity for much of the war, revived in preparation for the next General Election. With military victory in sight, Lloyd George and Law secretly decided, during the Summer, that a General Election, with the Coalition seeking to remain in power, would follow when hostilities ended. Britain, and her allies, completed the defeat of Germany, on November 11 1918, after more than four years of war.

7 Tranquillity

On November 14 1918, just three days after the end of World War One, the Coalition government called a General Election, to be held on December 14. Candidates who backed the Coalition were issued with a joint letter of support from Lloyd George and Bonar Law. This was dubbed the "Coupon" by Herbert Asquith, who saw the letter as being similar to wartime rationing coupons. The government's action in bouncing the nation into what became known as the "Coupon Election", immediately after the war, remained a source of controversary, and resentment, for many years. Indeed the event provided the starting point for a celebrated book, published a few months before the end of World War Two. This was Aneurin Bevan's *Why Not Trust the Tories?*

Bevan is famous as the Labour government minister who founded the National Health Service, which has been protecting the nation since 1948. Bevan was a staunch Socialist MP, for Ebbw Vale, involved in many controversies, between his first election to the Westminster Parliament in 1929, and his death in 1960. *Why Not Trust the Tories?* was published in 1944, and rapidly sold an amazing 80,000 copies. It was a brilliant critique of the methods of the Conservative Party, largely drawn from Bevan's observations across a quarter of a century of political activity. Nearly eighty years after it appeared, the book remains one of the most perceptive analyses of the negative outlook, and cynical actions, of the Conservatives. Much of the tragedy of the past has been repeated as farce in more recent times. Bevan's message should be heeded today, as a guide through the tangled web of Toryism.

Why Not Trust the Tories? was published by Victor Gollancz, in a series providing critiques of the Conservative, and right wing, approach that had dominated British politics in recent years. The most famous of these books was *Guilty Men*, by "Cato", published in 1940, attacking the appeasement of Fascism by the National Government. There was speculation that Bevan might be the author, but "Cato" was the pseudonym for a trio of journalists, including a young Michael Foot. Four years later, the title page of *Why Not Trust the Tories?* announced the author as "Celticus", but there was no need to speculate on the identity, as this was immediately followed by "(Aneurin Bevan, M.P.)". As a hardback, with a dust jacket, and a text running to 89 pages, this was a real book – weightier than a pamphlet.

With victory for Britain, and her allies, in World War Two, in sight, Bevan drew parallels with the position at the end of World War One. During both wars, Britain was governed by a coalition of the Liberal, Tory, and Labour parties. At the end of the first war, Labour decided to revert to independence, opposing a continued Coalition. The Tories, shunning Liberals loyal to Asquith, manoeuvered to ensure they emerged from the Election with more MPs than their partners, and thereby controlled the government moving forward. Among the instigators of the plan was Winston Churchill, a Liberal MP who was formerly a Tory, would later become a Tory again, and was Prime Minister at the time Bevan was writing.

The Coupon Unionists and Liberals fought the Election as an alliance, being joined by some Coalition Labour candidates, and also the National Democratic Party – the latter including defectors from Labour. The Coalition won a landslide victory, taking 482 out of the 707 seats, which was a majority of 257. The supporters of the Coalition consisted of 335 Unionists, 133 Coalition Liberals, 10 members of the National Democratic Party, and 4 Coalition Labour MPs. Meanwhile there were 48 non-Coalition Unionists. The largest opposition party was Sinn Fein, but its 73 MPs refused to take their seats. The Labour Party won 59 seats, the Asquithian Liberals 28 seats, and the others 17.

Bevan's book moves on to 1919, and looks at a British coal mining industry in a sorry state, due to mismanagement and profiteering by the owners. The miners were calling for nationalisation combined with workers' control. Lloyd George, on behalf of the Coalition government, set up a royal commission, chaired by John Sankey, an eminent lawyer, to examine the industry. Bonar Law, as Leader of the Tories, pledged to implement the recommendations, accepting these could include nationalisation. The Sankey Commission – persuaded by the miners and Labour Party – reported in favour of nationalisation. The Coalition government rapidly reneged on its promise. The coal mines remained in the hands of private owners, who were allowed to increase the price of coal, and the industry remained in crisis. Bevan noted that production dropped, from 286,000,000 tons in 1913, to 196,000,000 tons in 1943. In office from 1945, Labour brought the coal mines, and the steel industry, into public ownership.

Later conflict between the Tories and the miners led to the downfall of Edward Heath's government in 1974. Margaret Thatcher took power, in 1979, leading an ideological right wing government, which attacked the organised working class, with deindustrialisation and privatisation. The actions of Thatcher, John Major, and David Cameron would have shocked even Bevan. The protracted miners' strike of 1984-85 failed to reverse Tory decimation of the coal industry, which was privatised in 1994, and deep coal mining in Britain completely ceased in 2015. British steel was mostly denationalised by the Conservatives in 1953, renationalised by Labour in 1967, and then privatised by the Conservatives in 1988. Since 2010, the steel industry in this country, largely owned by foreign companies, has experienced a lot of uncertainty, with the Conservatives refusing suggestions that renationalisation be used to protect manufacturing capacity.

At the end of 1919, Nancy Astor, a Unionist, became the first woman MP to take her seat in the Commons. This merely represented the undemocratic nature of the Unionists, as Nancy was elected MP for Plymouth Drake, replacing her husband, Waldorf Astor, who had moved to the House of Lords. Waldorf became Viscount Astor, in succession to his father William Astor, originally a capitalist from the USA. William was admitted into the British peerage, as a reward for his financial contributions to the Unionist Party. Nancy Astor remained an MP until 1945, becoming notorious in the 1930s as a sympathiser of the Nazis, who frequently expressed anti-Semitic opinions. During the 2019 General Election campaign, a statue of Nancy Astor, was unveiled by Theresa May, in Plymouth, as the Tories continued to celebrate a dubious legacy.

Continuation of the Coalition after 1918 did not prove a success, with divisions between Liberals and Unionists. The government provided for Irish Home Rule in the Government of Ireland Act 1920, but six counties in Ulster were excluded, as a reward for the Unionist terrorist campaign prior to the First World War. Civil war in Ireland, between 1919 and 1921, was followed by the majority of the island becoming the Irish Free State in 1922, while Northern Ireland remained part of the United Kingdom. James Craig, a Unionist who had been a major conspirator in the Larne gun-running, became the first Prime Minister of Northern Ireland, in June 1921. The devolved Parliament, in Belfast, was to continue until 1972. A disillusioned Edward Carson spoke against the partition, in the House of Lords, during December 1921. Carson said "What a fool I was. I was only a puppet, and so was Ulster, and so was Ireland, in the political game that was to get the Conservative Party into power".

The majority of the Unionist Party began to look for an end to the Coalition. On the other hand, many Unionist MPs wished their alliance with the Coalition Liberals to become permanent. In March 1921, ill health forced Law's resignation from the government, and the Leadership of the Unionists. Some Unionists wanted Lloyd George to move for the Unionist Leadership, to unite the two wings of the Coalition, but Austen Chamberlain was unanimously elected by a party meeting. Chamberlain's main concern was to persuade the party that the Coalition was in its best interests, and should lead to merger. Continuation of the Coalition was harming the Unionist organisation, as party members became disenchanted. This was aggravated by the activities of the Party Treasurer, Lord Farquhar, a supporter of the Coalition, with a failing mind, who diverted Unionist Party money into the hands of Lloyd George.

During 1922, George Younger, the Unionist Party Chairman, led pressure within the party for an end to the Coalition. The government had struggled with problems, including high unemployment, and failure of the Cabinet to agree on a plan to reform the House of Lords. Lloyd George was damaged by Unionist outrage at his using the sale of honours to finance his political activities. The Unionists conveniently forgot that they also followed this practice. Realising their position was getting weaker, Unionists in the Cabinet came to favour a General Election. They believed that no party would win a majority, and the Coalition would continue in office. On October 10, the Cabinet decided to hold the Election as soon as possible. Unionist Party managers opposed this, and a split appeared likely. Chamberlain decided to call a party meeting, and attempt to assert his authority. At the Carlton Club, on October 19, Chamberlain set out his position in a poor speech, following which strong cases from Stanley Baldwin, the President of the Board of Trade, and Law, against continued Coalition were decisive. Balfour failed to move the meeting with a demand that the party follow its Leader. The meeting voted 187 to 87 in favour of ending the Coalition. This produced the immediate resignations of Chamberlain, as Unionist Leader, and Lloyd George, as Prime Minister.

George V asked Bonar Law to form a government. Law declined to accept the office of Prime Minister until he had been re-elected Leader of the Unionists. Law was unanimously elected Leader, on October 23, at an incongruous venue for such an event, the Hotel Cecil. Law had to form a government without Austen Chamberlain, Balfour, and their supporters. Baldwin was rewarded for his part in the downfall of the Coalition, with the post of Chancellor of the Exchequer. Law remains the only person to have two separate spells as the overall Leader of the Conservatives. With Law now taking the premiership, Austen Chamberlain, departing after only 19 months in post, was left as the first overall Leader of the party to fail to become Prime Minister. In recent times, William Hague, Iain Duncan Smith, and Michael Howard, three consecutive Conservative Leaders, across the years 1997 to 2005, have also missed out on taking the premiership.

Law sought a mandate in a General Election, set for November 15. Law wrote in the Unionist manifesto that the country needed "tranquillity". This was just what the party wanted, and it set out to persuade the electorate that it was what they should vote for. Conservatives have traditionally believed the political process should be accorded a limited value. This reflects their wish for a society in which people are not politically engaged, and ready to challenge the established order. Nothing positive was likely to result from tranquillity, but the Unionists won 344 seats, and a majority of 73. The Labour Party took 142 seats, the official Liberal Party 60, the National Liberals 57, and the others 12.

Looking back at the way in which the Tories ditched their failing alliance with the Liberals, pretending to offer a new start, Bevan concluded this was an example of continual deception. In a passage often quoted in the current day, Bevan wrote "Honest politics and Tory politics are contradictions in terms. Lying is a necessary part of a Tory's political equipment, for it is essential for him to conceal his real intentions from the people. This is partly the reason for his success in keeping power". The Coalition's delivery of economic depression, with mass unemployment, gave way to Tory "Tranquility", which proved to be another word for cuts to services, and more unemployment. The General Election of 1922 has been echoed in 2015, as the Conservatives gained marginal constituencies from their partners in a Coalition government, the Liberal Democrats, and won a majority in the Commons. In January 1923, Law threatened to resign, rather than accept terms Baldwin had agreed with the USA, in settlement of the UK's war debts. The Cabinet persuaded Law this would be a disaster, and he remained in office. Law released his frustration by writing a letter to *The Times*, signed "A Colonial Correspondent", attacking the deal his government decided to accept. Law was forced into retirement in May, by cancer of the throat, from which he was to die on October 30.

The king appointed Baldwin as Prime Minister, and the latter was elected Unionist Leader at a party meeting. Baldwin remained as Chancellor until July, when he handed the post to Neville Chamberlain, the half-brother of Austen. Baldwin believed tariffs were necessary to combat unemployment, and decided to call an Election on the issue. He hoped protection would reunite the Unionist Party, fearing that Austen Chamberlain, and his supporters, might ally with Lloyd George's wing of the Liberals to form a new party. Baldwin made a mistake in calling the Election, set for December 6, as the Unionists were unprepared. Baldwin's plan succeeded to the extent that Austen Chamberlain was reconciled, but it also aided reunification of the Liberal Party, which concentrated on defending free trade. The Unionists lost their majority, but were still the largest party, with 258 seats, ahead of Labour's 191, and the Liberals' 151, with the others winning 7 seats. In January 1924, the government was defeated in the Commons, on the king's speech, and resigned.

8 Appeasement

A minority Labour government was formed in 1924, with Ramsey MacDonald as Prime Minister. The Tories now moved away from calling themselves the Unionist Party, reverting to the Conservative Party name, as the Union with Ireland had been dissolved. On the other hand, in October 1924, the National Union became known as the National Union of Conservative and Unionist Associations. Ever since then, Conservative and Unionist Party has been used, as an alternative to the simple Conservative Party, with varying degrees of emphasis. The Labour government was weak, being dependent upon the Liberals. It fell following accusations that it forced the withdrawal of the prosecution of J R Campbell, a Communist, for an incitement to mutiny, for political reasons. With the Liberals refusing to support it, the government was defeated in the Commons, and Parliament was dissolved. Polling day in the Election was October 29.

The Tories concentrated on attacking the Labour Party, being helped by the appearance of the Zinoviev letter. This forged letter was alleged to have been written by the President of the Communist International, Zinoviev, to the British Communist Party, advising them on tactics. The Conservatives were able to obtain a copy of the letter due to links with MI5. Joseph Ball had recently joined the Central Office from MI5, taking on responsibility for Conservative propaganda. Publicity surrounding the letter harmed the Labour Party. The Conservatives won 419 seats, Labour 151, the Liberals 40, and the others 5.

Labour gave way to a Conservative administration, with Baldwin re-assuming the post of Prime Minister. Austen Chamberlain became Foreign Secretary, while Neville Chamberlain was Minister of Health. Churchill had been returned to Parliament, at the Election, as an Anti-Socialist Constitutionalist, having broken with the Liberals. Baldwin appointed him Chancellor of the Exchequer. This led to

Churchill rejoining the Conservative Party, although he delayed the fateful moment for another year. In April 1925, reconciliation in the party was completed, as Balfour succeeded Curzon as Lord President, on the death of the latter. Balfour, who had been created an Earl in 1922, was to be a member of the government for the remainder of its term in office.

The government followed a negative policy, and failed to deal with the nation's economic problems, with unemployment remaining at above one million people throughout its term in office. Churchill struggled as Chancellor, never being in control of the situation, or really understanding what he was doing. The government's refusal to alleviate the plight of the miners led to the Trade Union Congress organising a General Strike, during May 1926. Writing in 1944, Aneurin Bevan recalled that events since rejection of the 1919 Sankey report "reduced the miners to such a state of desperation and the coal industry to such bankruptcy that the owners felt compelled to insist on ferocious reductions in wages". The General Strike collapsed after nine days, but "the miners resisted for seven savage months", and Bevan pointed out that the Tory response was "a calamitous setback to industrial recovery for British industry generally". After the miners were forced back to work, the government followed up with the Trade Disputes and Trade Unions Act of 1927, to make political strikes illegal, and enforce a system of contracting in for the political levy. The latter element was a clear ruling class attack on the Labour Party, seeking to reduce its funding by working people, via their union membership. This legislation would be repealed by a 1946 Act, with the same title, carried by the Labour government of which Bevan was a member. Recent decades have brought a series of legislation from Conservative governments, reducing the strength and independence of the trade unions. These stretch from the Employment Act 1980, the year after Margaret Thatcher became Prime Minister, to the Trade Union Act 2016, passed a few weeks before David Cameron departed from office.

The Conservatives had supported Benito Mussolini's Fascist dictatorship, in Italy, ever since it took power in 1922. In a speech made in Italy, during 1927, Churchill celebrated Mussolini's actions, and said "If I had been an Italian, I am sure that I should have been whole-heartedly with you from the start to finish, in your triumphant struggle against the bestial appetites and passions of Leninism". Churchill went on to celebrate the "international aspect of Fascism" which "has rendered service to the whole world". Churchill thought that Fascism was defending "the honour and stability of civilised society", and providing "the necessary antidote to the Russian poison".

The Representation of the People Act 1928 equalised the franchise for men and women, at the age of 21, despite the opposition of the Conservative Party organisation to this. J C C Davidson, who became Party Chairman in October 1926, was assisted by Joseph Ball, and the latter organised infiltration of the Labour Party's headquarters. Davidson set about improving the Conservative Party's financial position, with the sale of honours to individuals largely being replaced by the obtaining of donations from companies. Ever since Davidson developed the process, company donations have dominated Conservative central funding. This has demonstrated that the Conservative Party is the party of capitalists, rather than the general population. In contrast to a recurring Conservative theme, that trade unionists' donations to the Labour Party should be restricted, there has been a striking absence of curbs on company donations to the Tories.

As its term in office progressed, the government became increasingly unpopular. Apart from extension of the franchise for women, its only achievement was a programme of social reform legislation, carried by Neville Chamberlain. Baldwin called a General Election, held on May 30 1929, fought on the uninspiring slogan "Safety First". Lacking a positive programme, the Conservatives concentrated on attacks on the other parties. Labour won 288 seats, the Conservatives 260, the

Liberals 59, and the others 8. Baldwin resigned, and a second minority Labour government was formed, with Ramsey MacDonald again Prime Minister.

The Conservative leadership saw part of the reason for their defeat in the lack of new policies. The Shadow Cabinet decided to set up a Conservative Research Department, and Neville Chamberlain became its Chairman, in March 1930. Two months later, Chamberlain was also appointed Party Chairman, having secured the resignation of Davidson, who was unpopular. Chamberlain carried out a scheme of reorganisation, and then resigned in 1931. The tariff issue returned to prominence and, as usual, caused problems. Baldwin faced pressure from supporters of tariffs, led by Conservative press barons, Lords Rothermere and Beaverbrook. This divided the party, and threatened Baldwin's position as Leader. Baldwin showed sympathy for the government's policies, where he agreed with them, including Labour plans for self-government in India. This caused Churchill to resign from the Shadow Cabinet, in January 1931. Labour faced the effects of a severe international capitalist crisis. As the economic situation deteriorated, MacDonald decided to form a coalition government, having secured the agreement of Baldwin and Chamberlain to this plan. On August 24 1931, MacDonald resigned as Prime Minister, thereby disbanding the Labour government, and was immediately reappointed by the king, allowing him to form a new administration.

The Conservatives and Liberals accepted the National Government, but MacDonald was only able to carry a minority of his colleagues, who founded the National Labour Party. Official Labour went into opposition. The early weeks of the government's term of office saw drastic measures, which dealt with the immediate financial crisis. The government held a quick General Election, with polling day being October 27, and won 554 seats – the Conservatives returning 473 MPs, the Liberals 68, and National Labour 13. The coalition majority was a massive 491, as the Labour Party won just 52 seats, and there were 11 other opposition MPs. MacDonald remained Prime Minister, displaying diminishing abilities, and Baldwin, acting as deputy, held effective control of the government. As Bevan later recalled, "it was Stanley Baldwin, and not the decoy Prime Minister, Ramsey MacDonald, who was the master of the political situation".

The government was generally to fail in economic terms, and unemployment was at above one million people through the remainder of the decade. Neville Chamberlain, as Chancellor of the Exchequer, carried the introduction of tariffs with Imperial Preference, in 1932. Although the eventual effect was of limited benefit, the Conservative Party was pleased to have finally secured tariffs. On the other hand, these taxes led to the resignation of several government ministers, and a split in the Liberal Party. National Liberals remained in the government, becoming dependent on the Conservatives, while the official Liberal Party joined the opposition.

In January 1933, Adolf Hitler, and the Nazi Party, seized power in Germany. The Conservatives were slow to realise the nature of the threat, as many of them, notably Winston Churchill, admired Hitler's nationalist approach. The Conservatives saw Fascism as preferable to democracy and Socialism. They realised that Fascism is merely an authoritarian version of Conservatism. The Conservatives sympathised with Sir Oswald Mosley's British Union of Fascists, which was formed in 1932. Churchill published a profile of Hitler, in 1935, which looked at disputes over disarmament of Germany, and had these words of praise for the Nazi leader: "Eventually, all that came out of the Disarmament conferences was the Rearmament of Germany. While all these formidable transformations were occurring in Europe, Corporal Hitler was fighting his long, wearing battle for the German heart. The story of that struggle cannot be read without admiration for the courage, the single-mindedness, and the personal force which enabled him to challenge, defy, overcome, or conciliate all the authorities or resistances which barred his path". The National

Government failed to pursue effective rearmament, as a result of complacency about the threat from Germany, and a wish to economise. Churchill belatedly understood the threat posed by Hitler, but he was an isolated figure in the Conservative Party, with few supporters. Austen Chamberlain was another critic of the government's foreign policy, from the backbenches, until his death in March 1937.

Ramsey MacDonald was increasingly unable to lead the government, as his health declined, and Baldwin became Prime Minister on June 7 1935. The government concluded an Anglo-German Naval Agreement, which provided for the limitation of the German navy in relation to the British navy. This conflicted with the government's support for the League of Nations, and collective security. An Election was held on November 14, and the National Government retained power, winning 429 seats, and a majority of 243. The Conservatives took 388 seats, the National Liberals 33, and National Labour 8. The Labour Party returned 154 MPs (a notable increase compared to 1931), the official Liberals 21, and the others 11. During the Election campaign, Baldwin said "I give you my word that there will be no great armaments". The following year, Baldwin told Parliament he had been in favour of rearmament, but not spelt this out at the time. Looking back, Bevan commented "When Baldwin admitted….that he feared the Tories would have lost the election if he had told the truth to the people, his Tory supporters were shocked, not because he had deceived the people but because he was loose-tongued enough to admit it. It was not his immorality they objected to, but his garrulity".

King George V died in January 1936, being succeeded by Edward VIII. Baldwin, suffering increasingly poor health, decided to remain Prime Minister, to help the new king, putting the Conservative Party's reverence for the monarchy before the interests of the British people. Baldwin was also motivated by the worsening of the international situation, but failed to take effective action in this respect. In March, Germany reoccupied the Rhineland, and the National Government declined to confront Hitler. In May, Italy completed the conquest of Abyssinia, and the Conservatives decided against the continuation of sanctions, agreed by the League of Nations, against Italy. In July, the Spanish Civil War was started by General Franco, leading an army revolt against the democratically elected Socialist and radical government. MI6 supported Franco, acting on behalf of the British governing class, who were concerned that a progressive government in Spain was not good for capitalism. The Conservatives signed an international non-intervention agreement in respect of Spain, but failed to secure its operation. This allowed Italy and Germany to support Franco's attempts to impose Fascism. The Spanish war was a clear struggle, in which international Fascism, enabled by the British Conservatives, sought to end democracy.

Baldwin's wish to support Edward VIII was complicated by the king's affair with Wallis Simpson, an American divorcee. Edward wished to marry Mrs Simpson, but was barred by law from doing so while he was king. He chose to abdicate, in December, to be free to marry. Baldwin handled the matter well, but it diverted the government from the deteriorating international position. Much of the work of the Prime Minister was now delegated to Neville Chamberlain, who had recently displayed complacency by letting his London house to the German Ambassador, Joachim von Ribbentrop. In December 1936, Henry "Chips" Channon, a Conservative MP, wrote in his diary about a discussion with Lord Halifax, the Leader of the House of Lords: "I had a long conversation with Lord Halifax about Germany and his recent visit. He described Hitler's appearance, his khaki shirt, black breeches and patent leather evening shoes. He told me he liked all the Nazi leaders, even Goebbels, and he was much impressed, interested and amused by the visit. He thinks the regime absolutely fantastic, perhaps even too fantastic to be taken seriously. But he is very glad that he went, and thinks good may come of it. I was riveted by all he said, and reluctant to let him go". After the abdication of Edward VIII, Baldwin remained as Prime Minister, to see the next monarch, George VI, settle into the role. Baldwin finally felt it was safe to leave office in May 1937, his retirement being accompanied by that of Ramsey MacDonald.

Neville Chamberlain became Prime Minister on May 28. Three days later he was elected Leader of the Conservative Party, proposed by Edward Stanley, Seventeenth Earl of Derby (grandson of the nineteenth century Prime Minister), and seconded by Churchill. For all his criticism of the government, Churchill was not prepared for a decisive break with the Conservative leadership. Rearmament gained momentum with the succession of Chamberlain, but his major preoccupation was the policy of appeasement of Germany and Italy. Anthony Eden, the Foreign Secretary, an equivocal supporter of appeasement, resigned in February 1938, following a dispute with Chamberlain. Eden was replaced by Lord Halifax, who was clearly pro-German. In March, Germany annexed Austria, and Chamberlain took no action to prevent this. He was more concerned with maintaining good relations with Italy, formalised in April with the Anglo-Italian Agreement, recognising Italy's conquest of Abyssinia. Continuation of appeasement received the support of the majority of the Conservative Party. There were prominent roles for Conservatives in British organisations which supported the Fascist leaders. The Anglo-German Fellowship promoted the ideas of the Nazis, while the Friends of Italy and the Friends of National Spain did the same for the Fascists of the respective countries. This stance by the British governing party demoralised the democratic forces in Italy, Germany, and Spain. Hitler wanted to follow annexation of Austria with that of Czechoslovakia. In September, Chamberlain twice went to Germany for discussions with Hitler. He thought Hitler was justified in wishing to annex the German-populated area of Czechoslovakia, and announced that Britain should not go to war over "a quarrel in a far away country between people of whom we know nothing". Hitler then agreed to a conference on the issue, bringing together the governments of Germany, Italy,

Britain, and France, at the end of September, in Munich. The Czechs were excluded but, on September 30, the conference agreed that Germany could annex the German-populated areas of Czechoslovakia, while the integrity of the remainder would be guaranteed by the Powers. Chamberlain returned to Britain, waving a piece of paper, on which was written a statement – drawn up after the main agreement – in which he and Hitler expressed the wishes of their countries to settle disputes by negotiation, and avoid war. Chamberlain announced he had secured "peace with honour" – a phrase Disraeli had used after the Congress of Berlin in 1878 – and "peace for our time". Chamberlain continued to prepare for a possible war, but hoped to prevent it. The Conservatives were content to see the people of Austria and Czechoslovakia condemned to suffer the tyranny of the Nazis. The minority of Conservatives who opposed appeasement lacked a coherent alternative. Churchill's criticism finally became more forthright, but the Conservative Party's antipathy meant he was still excluded from the government,.

At the end of February 1939, the National Government recognised Franco as the ruler of Spain, despite the fact that the legal government of Spain remained in existence. The Spanish Civil War was not to be finally decided in Franco's favour until a few weeks later. In March, Germany overran Czechoslovakia, and Chamberlain realised appeasement had failed. It looked likely that Germany would move against Poland. Chamberlain finally made a stand, giving the Polish government a guarantee of national independence. Hitler responded by renouncing the Anglo-German Naval Agreement. There followed an unenthusiastic attempt by the National Government to secure an alliance with the Soviet Union, deterred by opposition from many Conservatives. Germany reached a non-aggression pact with the Soviet Union, in August, and invaded Poland, at the beginning of September. After some hesitation, Chamberlain issued an ultimatum to Germany, on September 3, ordering them to withdraw from Poland or face war. The Germans did not respond so Chamberlain declared war that same day.

Chamberlain arranged the resignation of the National Government, which had completed its calamitous course. The administration's legacy could not be so easily wished away, as Britain faced a war for which it was not prepared. The Conservatives, the supposedly national party, had imperilled the nation.

9 Some Form of Gestapo

Britain's role in the coalition of Allies that defeated Fascism in World War Two remains a justifiable source of national pride, three quarters of a century later. The Fascism of Nazi Germany threatened to enslave Britain, and much of the world, with a systematic programme of racism and genocide. The Nazis – working with rulers of the other Axis Powers, Italy and Japan – posed an unprecedented threat to progress and human civilisation. Amidst celebration of the eventual British victory, there has too often been a tendency to forget – or sweep under the carpet – the incompetence, and often deliberate treachery, of members of the Conservative Party, and ruling class, who developed the policy of appeasement.

Neville Chamberlain formed a new government in September 1939, based around a small War Cabinet, and Winston Churchill was appointed First Lord of the Admiralty. In the following months, the government did not conduct the war effectively. A series of blunders culminated in the disaster of the Norway campaign, at the beginning of May 1940. Churchill was primarily responsible for this setback, but was to benefit politically as a consequence of failure. In the Commons debate on the event, Labour divided the House on an adjournment motion. The government's majority was reduced to 81, as opposed to the usual figure of over 200, with 33 Conservatives voting against the government, while 60 abstained. This represented the equivalent of a defeat for Chamberlain, who resigned as Prime Minister, but remained Leader of the Conservative Party. Churchill became Prime Minister, gaining the position for himself at the expense of Lord Halifax. Most Conservatives would have preferred Halifax, who remained sympathetic to the Nazis, and had recently supported attempts to negotiate peace with Hitler.

Churchill formed a coalition, which included members of the Labour and Liberal parties as well as the Conservatives. Despite being discredited, Chamberlain stayed in the Cabinet, as Lord

President. Victory seemed far away, with catastrophe in France, at the end of May, when allied troops had to be evacuated from Dunkirk. The Summer, and early Autumn, saw the British air success against the Germans, in the Battle of Britain. Ill health forced Chamberlain to leave the government, at the end of September. He also resigned the Conservative Leadership, and a meeting to elect Churchill was held on October 9. The Conservatives chose to overlook Churchill's past record, for he was the obvious successor to Chamberlain, who died on November 9. The Germans launched the Blitz, a sustained bombing of Britain, during the Autumn, and this was to last through to the following Spring. The Carlton Club was bombed on October 14. Nobody was killed, but the building was destroyed. The Club was subsequently moved to a building in St James's Street, where it has remained ever since. Britain did not make any notable progress in the conduct of the war at this stage, although Churchill's handling of strategy was superior to that of Chamberlain. On June 22 1941, Germany invaded the Soviet Union, and this reduced the effectiveness of Germany. Japan entered the war, on December 7, by attacking the United States fleet at Pearl Harbour. The USA in turn joined the war, being allied with Britain. In June 1942, Britain formed an alliance with the Soviet Union, which in turn led to an unlikely friendship between Churchill and Stalin. Churchill appeared to have a penchant for ruthless dictators. Churchill was able to lead Britain to victory in the war, but this was achieved at a terrible cost in human life. The eventual combined death toll for British service personnel and civilians in World War Two was around 500,000 people. Churchill was also a racist, with a particular hatred for the people of India. Churchill's decision to divert food away from the population of Bengal, and towards the British army fighting in the region, turned the Bengal Famine into an act of genocide, in which over two million Indian people died of starvation, during 1943. A century on from the Irish Famine, the Tories' British nationalism was responsible for a massive death toll in their Empire.

The next General Election, scheduled for 1940, was postponed several times, by Parliament, during the course of the war. The Conservative Central Office, and the central organisation of the National Union, continued to work fairly regularly, but the constituency associations fell into decline. There was some preparation for the future, with a Post War Problems Central Committee set up in 1941, with R A Butler as Chairman. The Conservatives' work on future policy was matched by a similar development in the government. This process began with the investigation into social security, by Sir William Beveridge, a Liberal minister. The Beveridge Report, published in December 1942, envisaged a comprehensive scheme of social security. The plan was originally due to come into effect in July 1944. Bevan, in *Why Not Trust the Tories?*, explains that Conservative MPs pretended to be enthused about popular reforms, but found ways to delay implementation, with official enquiries and reports, followed by detailed consideration from the government.

When the Beveridge Report was debated in the House of Commons, during February 1943, the Tories carried a motion welcoming it as an idea for "post-war reconstruction", defeating a backbench Labour amendment that called for "early implementation of the plan". Bevan, one of 119 MPs who voted for the amendment, writes that here was "The Tory variant of 'Jam yesterday, jam tomorrow, but never jam today'". This curious idea was borrowed from Lewis Carroll's *Through the Looking Glass, And What Alice Found There*. The White Queen offered Alice work as a maid, for "Twopence a week, and jam every other day", going on to say "The rule is, jam tomorrow and jam yesterday – but never jam today". Bevan quotes the speech by "Mr Willink, who is now Minister of Health". Henry Willink said "I am for improving the Beveridge Report", although "there are many features of the report which I do not wish to see implemented". Willink voted with his fellow Tories for delay. During the following months, Beveridge, and opposition MPs, regularly pressed the government for a commitment to progress, but were met by delaying statements from Churchill and others. Bevan points out that massive public enthusiasm for the scheme was replaced by disillusion, as the Tories "contrive to drown the wistful hopes of the people for social security in a torrent of words, specious promises and endless delays".

Churchill addressed the nation, in a March 1943 radio broadcast, about post-war prospects. Bevan heard Churchill planning a repeat of 1918, with a suggestion that defeat of Hitler be followed by a Four Year Plan of reconstruction, led by "a National Government comprising the best men of all parties who are willing to serve". Bevan remarks that "Political renegades always start their career of treachery as the 'best men of all parties' and end up in the Tory knackery". A White Paper on Employment Policy arrived on May 26 1944, aimed at improving the morale of soldiers, preparing for what proved to be the D-Day Allied landings, in Normandy, on June 6. Bevan satirises the White Paper at length, particularly the idea that "thermostatic control of employment" could see troops – hoping to settle in family homes, and stable employment, upon their return after the war – being converted into mobile labourers, hopping between locations and trades, evening out fluctuations in the temperature of failing capitalism. Bevan quotes from a speech he made, when the White Paper was debated in Parliament. He said of the plan, "It runs away from every major social problem. It takes refuge in tricks, strategies, and devices because it has not the honesty to face up to the implications of the social problems involved". Bevan was correct in his scepticism. Post-war Conservatism has brought continued mismanagement of the economy, leading to several spells of mass unemployment. The total number of people out of work exceeded three million at times during the premierships of Margaret Thatcher, in the 1980s, and John Major, in the 1990s.

Bevan remarks that, as British forces were abroad fighting the Nazis, the Tories were focusing on their own priority. He points out that "the private ownership of land and the right to do what they like with it have always been the holy of the holies for the Tories". From this stem issues over the provision, and affordability, of housing. Millions of new homes would have to be built to rectify a pre-war shortfall, that had been exacerbated by the destruction of bombing. Following a familiar pattern, the Tories set up a Royal Commission, and two Committees of Enquiry, rejected suggestions they did not like, and were still procrastinating as Bevan completed work on his book. Britain did get a massive programme of house building after World War Two, but this was not initiated by the Tories. Bevan mentions that, in 1944, Henry Willink pledged a post-war house building programme, which the former thought was far from sufficient. In practice, the man directing the programme was none other than Bevan, whose role as Minister of Health also included responsibility for housing. During Labour's post-war spell in office, a million council houses were built, to a higher quality standard than was previously in place. Council houses remained a central part of affordable housing in Britain until the decline began during the 1980s. The Thatcher government's ideological sales of council houses has fueled growth in house prices and rents, plus homelessness, the sad legacy of which afflicts potential owners and tenants, while a large proportion of current Conservative MPs are landlords.

Bevan concludes his book with a survey of the Tory outlook, reaching far back to the origin of this grim phenomenon. He does not regard Tories, as men and women, to be "worse than other people". He thinks that Tories have good private morals "whereas their public morals are execrable", with habitual telling of lies about their political motives. Bevan points out that "the traditional Tory does not look upon himself as the people's representative, because the Tory doctrine pre-dates the rise of modern democracy". The Tories sided with Mussolini, Hitler, and Franco in their attacks on democratic government. Bevan also draws attention to the way in which the Tories had blocked a role for Parliament in the organisation of the British economy, to protect their own position as representatives of the propertied class. He states "By refusing the state effective intervention in the economic activities of society, the Tory is a potential Fascist element in the community. By denying Parliament a vigorous economic life he condemns it to death". Necessity had led to an economic role for the state during the war, but Bevan pointed to signs that the Tories would seek to retain power with the help of "a freedom campaign", backed by "the Tory millionaire press", with propaganda against state regulation. This would enable a Tory to "be free once more to hunt in the jungle of economic competition". Bevan warned that the left must guard against "appearing to be the advocates of regimentation as opposed to freedom". Bevan highlighted the perennial problem for the Tories: "It is how to induce the many to vote the few back into power at each election. Or, to put it another way, how to persuade the poor to allow the rich to continue ruling". In our own day, Jeremy Corbyn has made the phrase "For the many not the few" into the Labour Party's mantra, and 2017 Manifesto title.

The Allied intervention in France, in June 1944, proved a decisive turning point in the war. From that time onwards the Allies made significant military progress. Germany surrendered on May 8 1945, ending the war in Europe. Churchill wished the Coalition to continue until Japan was defeated, an event not expected to occur until the following year. This was subsequently hastened by the USA dropping atomic bombs on Hiroshima and Nagasaki, in August 1945, deliberately killing a vast number of civilians, whereupon Japan surrendered. Churchill was trying to repeat the trick of 1918, seeking a Tory-dominated coalition going forward, but Labour members of the government pressed for an early Election, on party lines. Churchill saw this prospect would prevent the Coalition from functioning effectively, and accepted that the Election be held soon. He resigned on behalf of the government, on May 23, and was reappointed by the king to head a caretaker Conservative administration. The Tories believed they would win the Election, and remain in office. Polling day was set for July 5 but, with many electors abroad with the services, the count was delayed, and the results not announced until July 26.

Tory propaganda failed in the Election campaign. Churchill concentrated on attacking the alleged intentions of the Labour Party, claiming that it would not be able to implement its programme without "some form of Gestapo". This was a sickening reference to the Nazi secret police, from the man who had recently caused Indians to starve to death in the Bengal Famine. Churchill seemed to forget his government included Labour members. There was also Churchill's own pre-war enthusiasm for Fascism and Nazism. Labour pointed out that Churchill, as the leader of the nation, was different to the Leader of the Conservatives. The legacy of the decade since the 1935 Election led to a shift in opinion, away from the Conservative Party. In his 1944 book, Bevan suggested that the public were moving towards the left, and this proved true. Labour won 393 seats, and a majority of 146, as people voted for new hope. The discredited Conservative Party took only 198 seats in the 1945 Election – their smallest total between humiliating defeats by the Liberals in 1906, and Labour in 1997. The National Liberals returned 15 MPs, the official Liberals 12, and the other parties 22.

The Labour Party formed its first majority government, with Clement Attlee as Prime Minister, and Aneurin Bevan as Minister of Health. Labour carried a major programme of reform, delivering the welfare state, along with public ownership of the Bank of England, coal mines, railways, electricity, and gas. The Conservatives opposed this in Parliament, but did not carry out the type of campaign adopted against the Liberals, in the years prior to the First World War. The party realised it could not regain power through resistance to change. The defining achievement of Labour was the National Health Service, with Bevan being the architect.

In 1946, the Conservatives voted against the legislation to set up the National Health Service. Following this the British Medical Association attempted to derail introduction of the service. With Bevan standing firm, the NHS opened on July 5 1948. On the previous day, he addressed a Labour Party rally, in Manchester. Having previously given Tories the benefit of the moral doubt, Bevan – probably antagonised by recent events – now saw things differently. He contrasted the promise of the welfare state with the poverty suffered by working people, including himself, due to the past policies of the Conservatives. "That is why," Bevan said, "no amount of cajolery, and no attempts at ethical or social seduction, can eradicate from my heart a deep burning hatred for the Tory Party that inflicted those bitter experiences on me. So far as I am concerned, they are lower than vermin. They condemned millions of first class people to semi-starvation". The Tory press reacted with furious condemnation of Bevan's statement. Conservative Party members set up a Vermin Club, as a protest against Bevan, with a prominent member being Margaret Thatcher, an aspiring politician destined to lead an attack on the NHS decades later.

The Conservative Party rethought its approach, and organisation. Churchill played little role in this, and ran the Shadow Cabinet on an informal basis. It generally met at the Savoy Hotel, eating and drinking took precedence over discussion of politics, and the agenda of the meeting was often ignored. The change in party structure, at this time, reflected the Conservative Party's practice of only developing its organisation as a result of necessity, rather than from any positive belief in its value. Reorganisation began under the supervision of Ralph Assheton, Chairman at the time of the General Election. In 1946, the Conservative Political Centre was founded, with the aim of stimulating discussion among members of the party. This amounted to little of significance, as the leadership maintained a hold on policy. This situation has continued since the centre was replaced, by the Conservative Policy Forum, during a 1998 party reorganisation. Lord Woolton, who followed Assheton as Party Chairman during 1946, concentrated on increasing membership, and raising money.

The Conservative Party considered the possibility of changing its name, due to the reactionary connotations. There were suggestions that it should be become the Constitutional Party, the Unionist Party, or the New Democratic Party. The Constitutional idea seemed viable, given that the Conservatives have always prided themselves as defenders of the constitution. On the other hand, the party has always been opposed to giving Britain a written constitution, realising that to do so would formalise democracy, and the rights of the British people – hindering attempts to limit these gains. Unionist was outdated, having been discarded two decades earlier. New Democratic was inappropriate, as the Conservative Party was not new or democratic – indeed it existed to oppose such ideas. The possible change was a sign of troubled thinking. Eventually the party decided that change would do more harm than good. The Conservative Party had to conserve to justify its existence, and this applied to its own name as much as the structure of society.

Woolton decided to rename the party's opponents, declaring that Conservatives should refer to the Labour Party as the Socialist Party. He reasoned that Labour showed the party represented working people, but Socialist suggested a foreign ideological system. The Conservative Party regards itself as representative of the British political tradition. In practice, as a reactionary party, which fails to reflect the progressive side of British political history. The progressive element has led to the development of democracy in Britain, with the Tories and Conservatives setting themselves against the process. The Conservatives charge against Labour was unfounded, as the Labour Party does not derive solely from the continental Socialist movement. It equally has its roots in the tradition of British radicalism, and democratic struggle. That tradition is centuries old, and predates Toryism. The Labour Party is a people's party whereas, despite its claims, the Conservative Party represents the interests of the ruling class.

A few days after calling the 1983 General Election, Margaret Thatcher made a speech at the Scottish Conservative Party

Conference. Thatcher said: "This is a historic election. For the choice facing the nation is between two totally different ways of life. And what a prize we have to fight for, no less than the chance to banish from our land the dark divisive clouds of Marxist Socialism, and bring together men and women from all walks of life who share a belief in freedom, and who have the courage to uphold it". The mention of Marxist Socialism followed on from Thatcher claiming "Without a shadow of a doubt, this Labour Party has the most extreme and most damaging programme ever placed before the British electorate". One Labour policy highlighted by Thatcher was a plan to leave the European Economic Community, which she believed would put Scottish jobs and investment at risk. Britain was destined to leave the European Union in 2020, at the behest of the Tory Brexiteers, following a 2016 referendum in which most Scottish people voted to remain members.

The departure from the EU occurred a few weeks after the 2019 General Election. That campaign opened with Boris Johnson writing: "The tragedy of the modern Labour Party is that they detest the profit motive so viscerally – and would raise taxes so wantonly – that they would destroy the very basis of this country's prosperity. They pretend that their hatred is directed only at certain billionaires – and they point their fingers at individuals with a relish and a vindictiveness not seen since Stalin persecuted the kulaks". During the 1930s, Stalin ordered the killing of millions of landowners, known as the kulaks, in the Soviet Union. Comparing the Labour Party to Stalin was a disgraceful slur. It was also incredibly hypocritical, given that Johnson's political hero is Winston Churchill, a man who enjoyed good relations with Stalin during the latter part of World War Two. At the same time, Churchill caused the deaths of a massive number of Indian people in a famine.

The Conservative Party published *The Industrial Charter* in 1947. This was a defence of free enterprise, but also acknowledged the need for government intervention in industry. Churchill was not enthusiastic, and did not even read the charter, which was followed by similar documents dealing with agriculture, the Empire, Scotland, Wales, and women. In 1949, a full policy statement appeared, *The Right Road for Britain*. Belatedly showing an interest, Churchill wrote a Foreword, comparing the plan to his father's Tory Democracy, ignoring the fact that Randolph lacked a programme. An agreement, reached in 1947, between Lord Woolton, as Chairman of the Conservatives, and Lord Teviot, who held the equivalent role in the National Liberals, led to amalgamation of the party organisations. The official Liberal Party experienced a long period in the wilderness, after dissolution of the coalition in 1945. They did not return to power until 2010, when a Conservative and Liberal coalition government, following that of 1918 to 1922, pursued a policy of austerity, to condemn the hopes of a nation to the scrapheap.

In 1948, the National Union set up a Committee on Party Organisation, chaired by David Maxwell-Fyfe. The committee produced an Interim Report in 1948, and a Final Report in 1949. Nevertheless the Conservative Party structure remained essentially undemocratic, reflecting the nature of its political ideas. The organisation was dominated by the leadership, while the membership were denied any effective influence. Central Office remained responsible to the party Leader, who made the major appointments, and this body co-ordinated the work of the party. Conservative Central Office has retained a largely unchanged role since then, although it was renamed Conservative Campaign Headquarters in 2014. The National Union organised the Party Conference, but this gathering had no influence in setting policy, and its views were dismissed when they conflicted with the leadership. The rank and file accepted this, regarding the Conference merely as an opportunity to display adulation of their leaders. The membership of the Conservative Party have rarely sought to democratise the party's organisation and policy making. They have acquiesced in their own subordination, accepting that the Conservative Party is based on hierarchy.

The Labour government called an Election for February 23 1950. This was the first General Election to be held on a one person one vote basis, Labour having abolished the unfair system of plural votes – beloved of wealthy Tories – the previous year. The Election reduced the Labour majority to 5, as the party won 315 seats, compared to the Conservatives' 298, with the Liberals on 9, and the others 3. The Conservatives had staged a major recovery from their position in 1945, and were confident of regaining power before very long. Having a small majority, Labour held another Election, on October 25 1951. The Conservatives won 321 seats, Labour 295, the Liberals 6, and the others 3. The Conservatives had a majority of 17, although Labour had won the popular vote, with a massive endorsement of their radical programme, implemented during six years in office. Labour's poll of 13,948,385 was a higher vote than any party achieved at a British General Election prior to that date – indeed Labour's 1951 total would not be bettered by any party until 1992.

10 Thirteen Years of Tory Misrule

Winston Churchill reassumed the premiership in 1951, planning to only hold office for a few months, before passing the role to Anthony Eden, his Foreign Secretary. The Conservatives set out to prove that they had adapted to the post-war political reality. They believed they could manage capitalism better than the Labour Party, to provide increased prosperity, while maintaining the welfare state. R A Butler, the Chancellor of the Exchequer, played a major role in this, but in a rather haphazard way, as he did not have a firm grasp of economics. The government made great play of achieving its target of building 300,000 houses a year, but was only able to do so because it made housing a major priority at the expense of other policies. This programme was supervised by Harold Macmillan, the Housing Minister.

As the months passed, Churchill showed no sign of being ready to surrender his position. In February 1952, Elizabeth II succeeded George VI, and Churchill enjoyed working with the new monarch. Eden fell seriously ill, during March 1953, and Churchill became acting Foreign Secretary. At the end of June, Churchill suffered a stroke and, with Eden still unable to carry out his duties, R A Butler headed the government, while Lord Salisbury acted as Foreign Secretary. After a period of rest, Churchill work as Prime Minister, but he did not make a full recovery. Eden himself was sufficiently recovered by the Autumn to be able to succeed as Prime Minister, but this did not occur, with Churchill unwilling to take his leave of power. The Cabinet remained loyal to Churchill, but were doubtful whether he should continue as Prime Minister. Cabinet meetings degenerated into monologues from Churchill, but he was unable to take decisions. Churchill finally handed over the premiership in 1955, and left the government, but remained prominent until his death, in 1965.

Anthony Eden became Prime Minister on April 6 1955, and was unanimously elected Conservative Leader, by a party meeting on April 21. Eden called a General Election for May 25, the outcome of which was the Conservatives winning 344 seats, Labour 277, the Liberals 6, and the others 3. The Conservatives had increased their majority to 59, but many party members soon became disillusioned, feeling the government should start to dismantle the progressive achievements of Labour. In July 1956, Egypt nationalised the Suez Canal Company. In October, Eden organised a military operation, with France and Israel, aimed at capturing the canal, but international pressure forced Eden to abandon the campaign. The failure of the Suez expedition strained Eden's health, and in November he went to Jamaica to recuperate, staying at Goldeneye, the home where Ian Fleming wrote the James Bond books. Meanwhile Butler acted as the head of the government. Eden returned to Britain in December, planning to remain Prime Minister, but his health prevented this. On January 8 1957, Eden resigned the premiership, on medical advice – he also left the House of Commons.

The succession lay between R A Butler and Harold Macmillan. Consultations among the Conservative leadership demonstrated Macmillan was the more popular candidate, and the queen appointed him Prime Minister, on January 10. Macmillan was elected party Leader on January 22. The government had been badly shaken by the Suez disaster, but Macmillan provided strong leadership, and restored its position. Macmillan's main preoccupation was the maintenance of an expanding economy. In a speech at Bedford, on July 20, he said "Let's be frank about it, most of our people have never had it so good". Macmillan used the phrase as part of an attack on high wage claims, but unwittingly provided the Conservatives with a valuable slogan. During Macmillan's premiership the party propagandists were fond of telling the British people that they had "never had it so good". Conservatives were becoming increasingly worried about inflation. Peter Thorneycroft, Chancellor of the Exchequer, wished to attack inflation, by holding the money supply stable, with expenditure cuts. This was rejected by Macmillan, and the Cabinet, as it threatened to increase unemployment. The three Treasury Ministers, Thorneycroft, Enoch Powell, and Nigel Birch, resigned in January 1958.

The next General Election was called in September 1959, with polling on October 8. The Conservatives won 365 seats to Labour's 258, while the Liberals returned 6 MPs, and a single Independent Conservative was also elected. The Conservatives had won a third successive Election, and increased their majority to 100 seats. Macmillan subsequently embarked on a reorganisation of Britain's economic and foreign policies, with a plan to enter the European Economic Community being announced in 1961. Macmillan aimed to disband the Empire. Modernisation was also pursued, through government spending programmes to revive the economy. All of this was a major reorientation of Conservative policy. Macmillan was gradually able to win over the party to support of the EEC. Concern about decolonisation provoked opposition from a group within the party, called the League of Empire Loyalists. The League eventually broke with the Conservatives, linking with other right wing groups to form a Fascist party, the National Front.

In July 1962, Macmillan carried out a panic reconstruction of the government, which harmed his image. Many Conservatives believed their government was merely conducting a holding operation, within the confines of the post-war consensus. There emerged a dispute between the supporters of modernisation and those of retrenchment. In January 1963 General De Gaulle, the French President, vetoed Britain joining the EEC, ending Macmillan's plan to use accession as a major theme for the next Election. EEC entry was destined to occur a decade later, in 1973, overseen by Edward Heath, but Macmillan had unwittingly paved the way for decades of Tory in-fighting. Europe was an issue that would play a significant role in the departure of the next four Conservative premiers after Heath, namely Margaret Thatcher in 1990, John Major in 1997, David Cameron in 2016, and Theresa May in 2019.

During March 1963, it emerged that John Profumo, the Minister for War, had an affair with Christine Keeler, at a time when she in turn was possibly having an affair with Eugene Ivanov, a naval attache at the Soviet Union's embassy. Profumo initially denied an affair with Keeler, in a statement to the Commons. In June, Profumo admitted he had lied, and resigned as an MP. The government faced allegations about a possible breach of security. Macmillan had mishandled the question, lightly accepting Profumo's original denial. The scandal harmed the Conservative Party in another way. The details of Profumo's affair with Keeler were accompanied with revelations about the sexual activities of the ruling class, which suggested a decline in their morals. The survival of the government was in doubt for a time. The establishment's answer was to persecute Stephen Ward, the man who introduced Ivanov to Keeler. Having been recruited by MI5 to keep track of Ivanov, Ward was disowned, tried on trumped-up charges of living off immoral earnings, and convicted, in a terrible miscarriage of justice. The hounding of Ward drove him to commit suicide.

Having weathered the storm, Macmillan decided to remain Prime Minister, but was forced to resign, in October, due to ill health. R A Butler looked set to succeed Macmillan, but the latter was opposed to this. Following Macmillan's advice, the queen sent for Lord Home, the Foreign Secretary, but did not appoint him as Prime Minister, until he had an opportunity of discussing the matter with colleagues. Several Cabinet ministers initially refused to serve under Home, but most changed their minds, in the interests of the Conservative Party, and he became Prime Minster. Macmillan recovered, but played little active role in politics, before retiring at the next Election.

Home was the first peer to be Prime Minister since Lord Salisbury. He immediately renounced his peerage, but did not become a genuine commoner, for he remained a Knight of the Thistle, and took the name Sir Alec Douglas-Home. He won a By-Election, at Kinross and West Perthshire, with polling on November 8, and was then elected party Leader in the traditional manner. Douglas-Home was not really fit to become Prime Minister, as he was preoccupied by foreign affairs, and knew little about domestic politics. Back in 1938, as Parliamentary Private Secretary to Neville Chamberlain, Douglas-Home attended the Munich conference. His government developed modernisation plans, with increased public spending in areas that had been neglected. There was a belated realisation, among Conservatives, that their period in office had not achieved much. Douglas-Home delayed the next Election as long as possible, and it was finally held on October 15 1964. The Conservative Party claimed they had brought prosperity, which Labour threatened, with nationalisation. Labour responded with an alternative to "thirteen years of Tory misrule". Labour won 317 seats, the Conservatives 304, and the Liberals 9. Labour had a majority of 4, and Douglas-Home resigned, bringing a long, and unsuccessful, period of Conservative government to an end.

11 Rivers of Blood

A Labour Government was formed in October 1964, with Harold Wilson as Prime Minister. Election defeat led to some reorganisation of the Conservative Party, and in January 1965 Edward du Cann – previously a minister in the Macmillan and Douglas-Home governments – became Party Chairman. Following the fiasco of 1963, a feeling finally developed that a formal procedure should be established for the election of the Leader. There had not previously been any pressure for this, given the anti-democratic outlook of the party. Alec Douglas-Home set up an election procedure, and the rules were adopted by the party in February 1965. Voting would be confined to Conservative MPs. To win on the first ballot, a candidate would require an overall majority equivalent to 15 per cent of those voting. On the second ballot a simple majority would suffice. The old process for choosing a Leader was not entirely dispensed with. The rules provided that the winner of the election would subsequently be confirmed as Leader by a party meeting. In the following months, a number of MPs set about attempting to secure the replacement of Douglas-Home, prompting him to resign on July 22. The Conservative Party's first genuine Leadership election featured three candidates, Edward Heath, Reginald Maudling, and Enoch Powell. The ballot was held on July 27, when Heath received 150 votes, Maudling 133, and Powell 15. Although Heath had not won the requisite majority, Maudling and Powell both withdrew from the contest, following which Heath was proclaimed Leader, at a party meeting on August 2. The Conservatives were now carrying out a major rethink of their policies. The process culminated with a statement, *Putting Britain Right Ahead*, being published in the Autumn, to coincide with the Party Conference. The main theme was economic growth, through policies of lower taxation, reduced government expenditure, legislation to reduce the strength of trade unions, and planned membership of the EEC.

Wilson called an Election for March 31 1966, seeking to increase the government's majority. Labour won 363 seats, the Conservatives 253, the Liberals 12, and the others 2. Labour had won a majority of 96 seats. The Conservative Party responded to defeat with a further development of their organisation and policy. Heath had been intent on sacking du Cann – who he did not like – as Party Chairman from the outset of his Leadership. Eventually differences between Heath and du Cann led to the latter resigning in 1967. The policy exercise continued throughout the Conservatives' period in opposition. The basic policy lines featured in the 1965 document were developed, and the emphasis remained on economic growth. Heath faced a challenge from the right wing of the party, for whom Enoch Powell emerged as the main spokesman. Powell served in the Shadow Cabinet, as Defence Spokesman, but developed an increasingly independent line. He did not support Britain's retention of nuclear weapons, and stated so publicly, differing from the vast majority of the Conservative Party. Powell argued that Britain's national identity had to be defined, and protected from threats, posed by immigration and the EEC. In April 1968, Heath dismissed Powell from the Shadow Cabinet, after the latter made a speech attacking immigration, claiming that racial tension could lead to "rivers of blood". The right saw that Powell was attacking the post-war political consensus, allowing a new Conservative approach to replace it. They believed that the party needed something more substantial than Heath's economic policy, if it was to regain power. The right were also concerned by Heath's support for the modernisation theme, introduced by Macmillan. They argued modernisation had not proved itself, and that the Conservatives should only follow policies that experience had shown to be successful. The right sought support through an assertion of traditional Conservative concerns. The leadership saw this as a possible threat to the party's new strategy, and an electoral liability. Nevertheless the right's arguments gained support in the party, with the result that the leadership made concessions. In the longer term, Powell's anticipation of what came to be known as monetarism, with resignation from Macmillan's government in 1958, was to influence the economic policies of Margaret Thatcher's government, from 1979 onwards. Long after his death, in 1998, Powell was also a figurehead for the racist element in the Conservative membership. The prejudices of these people led to the anti-immigration, "Hostile Environment", policy of Theresa May, a Tory Home Secretary, who became Prime Minister in 2016.

The next General Election took place on June 18 1970. The Conservatives, campaigning on the programme developed in opposition, won 330 seats, Labour 287, the Liberals 6, and the others 7. Heath became Prime Minister, with a Conservative majority of 30, while Alec Douglas-Home was Foreign Secretary for the second time, but Powell was excluded from the government. Victory united the party, and the disputes of the past few years ended. The government was initially intent on implementing its programme. At the Party Conference, in October, Heath said that the government would "embark on a change so radical, a revolution so quiet and so total that it will go far beyond the programme of a Parliament". It was a sign of how far the Conservatives had been forced to compromise their beliefs. The Conservative Party supposedly existed to block change, even change which fell far short of revolution.

A planned reduction of government intervention in industry was initially adhered to, while the Industrial Relations Act 1971 attacked the position of the unions. Heath's major aim was to achieve entry to the EEC, the negotiations for which led to the signing of a treaty of accession in January 1972, subject to the passing of legislation by Parliament. The Conservative Party was still not wholly in favour of EEC membership, and the European Communities Act was only carried with support of a minority of Labour MPs. Another major constitutional measure, the Local Government Act 1972, reorganised the structure in England and Wales. Many traditional counties were either rearranged or abolished, while new ones were created. March

1972 brought a resumption of direct rule of Northern Ireland, in response to the escalation of political violence there. The Ulster Volunteer Force, the Tory terrorists from the early twentieth century, had re-formed in 1966, to oppose the campaign for civil rights by Catholics. During 1972, the unemployment total reached more than one million people. With no sign of industry reviving as a result of the government's policies, it adopted intervention.

Entry into the EEC occurred on January 1 1973. Heath saw this as a major economic benefit for Britain. In return, he was prepared to accept the loss of Britain's independence. The laws of Britain ceased to be the sole preserve of its Parliament, as they became subject to those of the EEC. The government's economic strategy failed to produce successful results. November brought strikes by the miners and power workers. The miners' strike lasted through the Winter, and led to a three day working week. Heath had to choose between calling an Election, on the issue of who should govern the country, and the alternative of conceding to the miners. Heath decided upon an Election, set for February 28 1974, but the Conservatives intended to settle with the miners if they retained office. Powell, who had been a Conservative MP since 1950, denounced the Election as fraudulent, refused to be a candidate, and announced he would vote for the Labour Party, as it planned to hold a referendum on EEC membership. Labour won 301 seats, the Conservatives 297, the Liberals 14, the Ulster Unionists 11, and the others 12. The Ulster Unionists had broken with the Conservative Party, following disagreement over the governance of Northern Ireland.

Heath stayed in office, and attempted to form a coalition. The dubious decision to allow this, after Labour had won more seats than the Conservatives in the Election, was made by the queen, after consulting anonymous advisors. Heath's negotiations with the Liberals broke down, over their insistence on proportional representation, and he resigned on March 4. Harold Wilson formed a minority Labour government, and a second General

Election was held on October 10. With the Conservatives in a weak position, Heath was reduced to arguing in the campaign for a national, and not necessarily Conservative, government. Labour increased their number of MPs to 319, which gave them a tiny majority of 3 in the Commons, while the Conservatives had 277 seats. The Liberals had 13 seats, and the minor parties 26. The latter included 6 Ulster Unionists, one of whom was Enoch Powell, an Englishman who had become a strong supporter of Northern Ireland's place in the United Kingdom, and would remain an MP until 1987. At the time of the 1990 Conservative Leadership election, Powell pledged to rejoin the party if Margaret Thatcher won, but that did not happen. Returning to late 1974, with Heath having led the party to defeat in three out of four General Elections, there was talk of his position being challenged. The 1965 rules did not lay down that the Leader had to present themself for re-election, but Heath realised this was necessary, to retain authority. Heath announced he would hold an election, once the rules had been reviewed.

12 Thatcherism

The Conservative Party agreed new rules for its Leadership elections in January 1975, after Sir Alec Douglas-Home presided over a committee to consider the process. Contests could now be annual, if there was a challenger to the incumbent. The party's MPs remained as the electorate, but the required margin to win on the first ballot was increased, to 15 per cent of those entitled to vote. If this was not met, there would be a second ballot, and victory would require a candidate to have a majority over the combined votes of the other candidates. New candidates could join on the second ballot, the aim being to allow a supporter of Heath to enter, if he was defeated on the first ballot. If the second ballot did not produce a result, a third round would be held, between the three candidates who had secured the most votes at the second stage. The third ballot would feature voting by the Single Transferable Vote, ensuring an absolute majority for the winner.

The main threats to Heath seemed to be Edward du Cann and Keith Joseph, the latter of whom was Secretary of State for Health and Social Services in Heath's government. Du Cann decided against standing, and Joseph withdrew, in order to support Margaret Thatcher, who had been Education Secretary. Her candidacy was a surprise, given the male dominance of the Conservative Party. In the first ballot, on February 4, Thatcher won 130 votes, Heath 119, and Hugh Fraser (a backbencher) 16. Heath withdrew, and a second ballot was held on February 11, in which Thatcher took 146 votes, William Whitelaw 79, Geoffrey Howe 19, James Prior 19, and John Peyton 11. Thatcher became the first woman to lead a British political party.

Thatcher left the Shadow Cabinet largely unchanged, but Heath declined an offer to remain a member. Thatcher was appointed an honorary member of the Carlton Club, as membership was restricted to male Conservatives, but the Club did not wish to exclude the party Leader. The Carlton avoided the obvious step of opening membership to women – only making that change in 2008. Thatcher appointed Lord Thorneycroft as Party Chairman. Thorneycroft's resignation in 1958 gave him a reputation for supporting monetarism, the economic policy Thatcher favoured. A new course for the party, based on the ideas of the right, was set out in a 1976 policy document, *The Right Approach*.

The Labour government renegotiated the terms of Britain's EEC membership, and submitted the deal to a referendum, held on June 5 1975. The outcome was a vote for Britain remaining in the EEC, with improved terms, by a margin of 67 per cent to 33 per cent. Thatcher and the Conservatives campaigned for Britain to stay in the EEC, being consistent with their recent administration having arranged entry. Tony Benn, a radical member of the Labour government, had persuaded his Cabinet colleagues that the decision on membership should be delegated to the people, in a referendum. Benn was one of the most articulate advocates of Britain leaving the EEC, and continued to be influential in this cause through until his death, in 2014. To some extent, the decision of the British people to leave the European Union, in the second referendum, held by the Tories in 2016, was a posthumous victory for Benn's case.

Despite a small majority, the Labour government survived, helped by a pact with the Liberals, from March 1977 to August 1978. It looked likely that an Election would be held in the Autumn of 1978, but in September James Callaghan, who replaced Wilson as Prime Minister in 1976, announced there would not be an Election that year. The delay pleased the Conservatives, who believed they would be more likely to win an Election the following year. There followed "The Winter of Discontent", during which union opposition to the government's pay policy brought major disruption, aggravated by severe weather. The government was weakened by its failure to carry devolution for Scotland and Wales, and the Scottish National Party wanted a General Election. Taking advantage of this,

Thatcher moved a Commons motion of no confidence, on March 28 1979, and the government lost by one vote.

During the General Election campaign, the Conservative Party concentrated on Labour's troubled time in office. The Conservative manifesto had an unlikely title, *Time For a Change*. Polling took place on May 3, and the Conservatives won 339 seats to Labour's 269, while the Liberals took 11 seats, and the other parties 16. The Conservatives had a majority of 43, and Margaret Thatcher became Prime Minister. Thatcher's government initially represented a balance between adherents of her approach and sceptics. She excluded Edward Heath, who was to be a constant critic in the following years. A month after the Westminster election, the Conservatives won the first British election to the European Parliament, taking 60 seats to Labour's 17, while the other parties won 4 seats.

Thatcher proclaimed herself a "conviction politician", opposed to consensus. Her major preoccupation was an attempt to reverse Britain's long-term economic decline through monetarism. This was developed by Milton Friedman, an economist from the USA. Monetarism was a theory that had only been properly tested by one of the world's most barbaric regimes, the Fascist military dictatorship in Chile, and the result had been a spectacular failure. General Pinochet, the President of Chile, seized power in a military coup in 1973, with backing from the USA, removing a democratically elected Socialist government, led by Salvador Allende. Pinochet promptly directed his army to carry out a massacre, murdering countless thousands of people, just because they were Socialists, or trade unionists. In 1973, the government of Edward Heath – in which Thatcher was a Cabinet Minister – was one of the first in the world to recognise the Pinochet regime as supposedly legitimate. Monetarism was one element of a wider strategy introduced by Pinochet, as an extreme free market economic model was implemented, by an authoritarian state apparatus, in an overtly nationalist atmosphere. The term Neoliberalism was developed to describe the horrors of the

Chilean experiment. It was a strange phenomenon, and a contradiction in terms. Neoliberalism suggested a new form of liberalism, based on the economic side, but the political setting was far removed from this. Pinochet was a friend, and echo, of General Franco, the dictator of Spain, the country that was once colonial ruler of Chile. Franco retained power until he died in 1975, fully 39 years after the British elite backed his rebellion against democracy. Neoliberalism was reflected in the policies of Thatcher's, and her closest ally, Ronald Reagan, the Republican President of the USA from 1981 to 1989. Pinochet's spell in power ended in 1990, a few months before Thatcher departed from office, as the Chilean people restored their democracy.

Thatcher's government soon proved a calamity for Britain, with an economic strategy of reduced public expenditure, reduced taxation – especially for the ruling class – an attack on the trade unions, and the sale of public assets. When Thatcher took power, more than a million people were unemployed. This number increased to two million people in August 1980, and three million in January 1982. Thatcher's administration was authoritarian, inflexible, and callous. It attacked the democratic rights of the British people, notably with increased power for central government, and restrictions on local authorities, breaking here with a Conservative tradition. Thatcher followed an aggressive foreign policy, involving hostility to the Soviet Union, and was involved in constant disputes with the European Economic Community. Thatcher's rigid defence of what she perceived to be British interests within the EEC, an organisation founded by the Treaty of Rome, resulted in her frequently being referred to as a modern-day equivalent of Boadicea. Thatcher notably failed to improve the position of women, and her role as the first woman to lead the Conservatives was anomalous, as the party has perpetuated male dominance of British society. Strong belief in ideology placed Thatcher outside the mainstream of Conservatism. Thatcherism was proclaimed by supporters as radical, but it was a reactionary attack on progressive institutions. Thatcher's policies provoked opposition within the Conservative Party, but she called her opponents "wets", gradually removing sceptics from the government. Thatcher's annual speech, at the Party Conference, prompted the pathetic spectacle of marathon standing ovations.

The government became increasingly unpopular, until its fortunes were revived by victory in the Falklands War. The Argentinian invasion of the Falklands, in April 1982, represented a crisis. Thereafter the military operation to recover the islands reflected well on Thatcher. She dishonestly presented the war as a fight against Fascism, having previously allowed the sale of armaments to the military dictatorship of Argentina. It was only when these armaments were being used against Britain that Thatcher saw a problem. Nevertheless this surprise did not provoke Thatcher into opposition to Fascism, as during the war against Argentina she worked in alliance with the Pinochet regime in Chile.

The Conservatives were helped by changes in the Labour Party. Michael Foot replaced James Callaghan as Leader in 1980, while Tony Benn, and the radical left, became a major influence. A group of MPs on the right of the Labour Party formed the Social Democratic Party, at the start of 1981. The SDP subsequently worked with the Liberal Party, in an Alliance, which took a huge number of votes off Labour at the next Election, held on June 9 1983. The Conservatives won 397 seats, Labour 209, the Alliance 23, and the others 21. The Conservative majority of 144 was deceptive, with the party's 42 per cent share of the vote being little higher than the 40 per cent obtained in their massive defeat, by Labour, in 1945.

Thatcher's second term was as unsuccessful as the first. Cecil Parkinson, who had recently relinquished the post of Party Chairman, resigned from the government, in October 1983, with the revelation that his former secretary, Sara Keays, was expecting their child. Conservative central government limited local authorities' right to set their own rates, and abolished the

Greater London Council plus the Metropolitan County Councils – each of which were Labour-controlled. The miners went on strike during March 1984, in opposition to the Conservative programme of closing coal mines – part of a wider attack on industry, and the trade unions. For a whole year, the government was to preside over this damaging dispute, without attempting to settle it. British Telecom was privatised, the Tory word for the sale of public assets, in 1984. It was subsequently revealed that Keith Best, a Conservative MP, made multiple applications to buy shares in British Telecom, using minor variations on his name, and he was imprisoned for fraud in 1987. Best was soon released from prison, having argued that this sentence was too harsh, but a disproportionately low fine was increased. Following its re-election, the Thatcher government attacked the public service principles of the NHS, forcing the outsourcing of hospital cleaning, catering, and laundry to private companies.

The Conservatives lost ground in a European Parliament election, held in June 1984, but emerged as the largest party, with 45 seats, while Labour won 32 seats, and the other parties 4. Later that month, Thatcher negotiated a rebate on Britain's contribution to the EEC budget. Following this, Thatcher temporarily adopted a more positive approach, playing a major role in a 1986 agreement on the principles of a European Single Market. Ironically the majority of the Conservative Party would turn against this legacy, and withdrawal from the Single Market became a central aim of Brexiteers, following the 2016 EU referendum.

Thatcher narrowly escaped an assassination attempt, in October 1984, as the Irish Republican Army bombed the Grand Hotel, in Brighton, at the time of the Conservative Party Conference. Five members of the party were killed, including Anthony Berry, Deputy Chief Whip in the government. Nearly six years later, there were two further IRA attacks on the party. In June 1990, the Carlton Club was bombed, and Lord Kaberry, a former MP, suffered severe injuries, which led to his death the following year. Ian Gow, a sitting MP, was killed by a car bomb in July 1990.

The government discarded monetarism, during the Autumn of 1985, realising it had failed, but maintained its general plan. At the beginning of 1986, two Cabinet Ministers, Michael Heseltine and Leon Brittan, resigned amidst a dispute over the ownership of the Westland helicopter company. Thatcher's position appeared threatened by revelations about her disregard for Cabinet government, but she survived the crisis. Later in the year, the Conservatives were damaged by another scandal. This featured Jeffrey Archer, who had previously been a Conservative MP and successful businessman, only to lose a fortune, and abandon his political career. Archer had retrieved his fortune with large sales of a series of mediocre novels, and been appointed Deputy Chairman of the Party. Having rehabilitated himself, Archer's dealings with Monica Coghlan, a prostitute, were publicised, and the outcome was Archer's resignation. The following year, Archer dishonestly won £500,000 damages from the *Daily Star*, in a libel case about the scandal.

Thatcher visited the Soviet Union, early in 1987, with relations having thawed. A trip to the Soviet Union was an unlikely way for a Leader of the Conservative Party to improve their electoral prospects, but that was one of its aims. Thatcher called a General Election for June 11, and issued a Conservative manifesto entitled *The Next Moves Forward*. In the Foreword, Thatcher made the curious claim that her government was fulfilling the "One Nation" ideal. Thatcher led a poor campaign but, with the opposition weak, the Conservatives won 375 seats, Labour 229, the Alliance 22, and the others 24. The Conservatives retained power with a majority of 100 seats. Reconstruction of the government included the sacking of John Biffen, who had been Leader of the House of Commons. Biffen responded by saying that Thatcher's government was Stalinist. As Thatcher entered her third term in office, the thinking of the Conservative Party was characteristically incoherent.

Thatcher continued the sale of state assets to the private sector, including British Steel, British Leyland, and the water supply. This remained part of the wider, free market, economic policy, led by Nigel Lawson, Chancellor of the Exchequer since 1983. Lawson oversaw some reduction of unemployment, but inflation and interest rates both increased. Thatcher became increasingly agitated about developments in the EEC, and was opposed to Britain joining the European Exchange Rate Mechanism. Thatcher made a high-profile speech in Bruges, during September 1988, setting out her Eurosceptic approach. In June 1989, the Conservatives were defeated in the European Election, being reduced to 32 seats, while Labour won 45 – the other parties returned 4 MEPs between them. This was the Conservatives' first defeat in a General Election or European Election since 1974. Lawson, who favoured membership of the ERM, resigned as Chancellor in October 1989, feeling that Thatcher was undermining him. In November, Sir Anthony Meyer, a veteran backbench MP, challenged Thatcher for the Conservative Leadership. Meyer, who was pro-European, saw himself as a "stalking horse", hoping that his action would prompt a more high-profile MP to stand against Thatcher, but nobody else had the courage to do so. Thatcher won the contest by 314 votes to 33, but one sixth of the Conservative MPs either voted against her or abstained.

In the Spring of 1990, the Community Charge, trialed in Scotland a year earlier, was extended to England and Wales. This flat-rate charge, on local government electors, immediately became known as the Poll Tax. There was widespread public protest against the unfair nature of the charge, and an anti-Poll Tax riot in London. Throughout her premiership, Thatcher undermined the NHS, making clear a preference for private health. The National Health Service and Community Care Act, passed in June 1990, introduced a wide internal market to the NHS. This paved the way for future privatisation of large parts of the service, with 2012 legislation from the government of David Cameron a particularly significant step.

Britain joined the ERM, in October 1990, on the initiative of John Major, the Chancellor of the Exchequer, although Thatcher remained a sceptic. The following month, Geoffrey Howe, the Deputy Prime Minister, resigned from the government, and made a speech in the House of Commons attacking Thatcher's style of leadership. This prompted Michael Heseltine to challenge Thatcher for the Leadership. In the first ballot, on November 20, Thatcher beat Heseltine by 204 votes to 152, but fell four votes short of the 15 per cent majority needed for outright victory. Thatcher announced an intention of proceeding to the second ballot, but was persuaded by Cabinet colleagues that she had lost the confidence of the Parliamentary party. Thatcher withdrew from the contest on November 22.

John Major and Douglas Hurd, the Foreign Secretary, entered for the second round, on November 27. Major took 185 votes, Heseltine 131, and Hurd 56, a result that left Major two votes short of the required margin for victory, but the other two contestants withdrew. Major was declared Leader of the Conservative Party and, on the following day, appointed Prime Minister, by the queen. Major included Heseltine in his government, as Secretary of State for the Environment, tasked with finding a replacement for the Poll Tax, while Hurd remained Foreign Secretary. Thatcher returned to the backbenches, with her 11 years in power having ended in humiliation. The awful policies of Thatcherism, and Conservatism, would continue to damage Britain for a lot longer.

13 The Nasty Party

Within a few weeks of John Major becoming Prime Minister, he took Britain into the Gulf War, committing the armed forces to support the USA, in attacking Iraq, at the start of 1991, following the Iraqi invasion of Kuwait the previous year. An international coalition, led by the USA, defeated Iraq in the war, and liberated the Kuwaiti oil fields, for the benefit of the western world. At home, Europe remained a major issue, with formation in 1991 of the Anti-Federalist League, a pressure group which opposed European integration. The Conservatives carried legislation to replace the Poll Tax with the Council Tax – the latter took effect in 1993, gaining acceptance as a fairer means to finance local government. A General Election was held in April 1992. For much of the campaign it appeared likely that Labour would win, but John Major and the Conservatives retained power. The Conservatives won 336 seats, Labour 271, the Liberal Democrats 20, the Ulster Unionist Party 9, and others 15. The Conservatives' majority was reduced to 21 seats, although the party's vote of 14,093,007 surpassed that of Labour in 1951 as the highest yet for a single party.

In September 1992, currency speculation forced the withdrawal of Sterling from the ERM. Major's government struggled through the next few years, weakened by divisions over Britain's role in the EEC, which evolved into the European Union. There was also mismanagement of the economy, and unemployment increased to above three million people, in February 1993. A few months later, Major narrowly avoided defeat in the House of Commons over the European Union Maastricht Treaty, due to the "Maastricht Rebels" group of Conservative MPs. In his frustration, Major was overheard telling a television interviewer, when he thought the microphones were off, about the problems caused by "bastards" in his Cabinet. The United Kingdom Independence Party (UKIP) now replaced the Anti-Federalist League, and several "Maastricht Rebels" subsequently joined that party.

Sleaze and scandal led to a series of ministerial resignations. David Mellor, Secretary of State for National Heritage, departed in 1992, following revelations of his affair with Antonia de Sancha, an aspiring actress. Mellor was also damaged by circulation of knowledge that he took a holiday with Mona Bauwens, the daughter of Jaweed al-Ghussein, financier for the Palestinian Liberation Organisation, a couple of years earlier – Bauwens paid for the holiday. This was followed in 1993 by the resignation of Michael Mates, a minister in the Northern Ireland office, whose career dropped to a low-point due to support for Asil Nadir, a fugitive businessman. At the Conservative Party Conference, in October 1993, Major called for a "back to basics" campaign, the idea being that the Conservatives could lead Britain back to traditional values, based around decency, courtesy, and the family. It was an audacious move by Major, who previously had an affair with Edwina Currie, a fellow Conservative MP, which lasted from 1984 to 1988, but somehow remained secret until Currie revealed all, when publishing her diaries in 2002. A further significant outbreak of Tory sleaze, and corruption, would be exposed from 2017 onwards, during the premierships of Theresa May and Boris Johnson.

The Conservatives were heavily defeated in a European Union election, in June 1994, winning only 18 of the 87 seats across the United Kingdom. Labour won 62 seats, during the interim Leadership of Margaret Beckett, following the death of John Smith, who had replaced Neil Kinnock as Leader in 1992. Tony Blair was elected Labour Leader in July 1994, and set about a re-branding of the party, which reduced its Socialist commitment. During October, Tim Smith and Neil Hamilton resigned from the government, as it was revealed they had received cash to ask questions in the House of Commons, when they were backbenchers. Hamilton was embroiled in legal action stretching across several years, lost his seat in Parliament at the next General Election, and subsequently joined UKIP. In 1995, John Major called a Conservative Leadership election, in view of party intrigues against him, and defeated the challenger, John Redwood, by 218 votes to 89. The government's Commons majority was gradually eroded, due to By-Election defeats, along with the withdrawal of the whip from rebellious MPs, leading to the Conservatives being placed in a minority from 1996. Major delayed calling a General Election until the end of a five year term.

In May 1997 Labour won a General Election, with 419 seats, and a majority of 179, ending 18 years of Conservative rule, and starting a new era in British politics. The Conservatives were reduced to 165 seats, their smallest total since 1906. The Liberal Democrats won 46 seats, the Ulster Unionists 10, and the others 19. Major resigned as Conservative Leader, and a contest to replace him was held in June. William Hague became the youngest ever leader of the Conservatives, at the age of 36, beating Kenneth Clarke by 90 votes to 72 in the third ballot, following the elimination of Michael Howard and John Redwood, plus the withdrawal of Peter Lilley. The Labour government, led by Tony Blair, took office pledged to carry out a wide-ranging programme of reform. Labour achieved a great deal, defeating Conservative attempts to halt progress, while William Hague failed to give a strong lead to the latter party. Hague's attempt to modernise their image included a comical visit to a theme park, with his Chief of Staff, Sebastian Coe – previously an Olympic athlete and Conservative MP. Hague carried out some reorganisation of the Conservative Party, which led to it agreeing a formal constitution, in 1998, at which point a National Conservative Convention replaced the National Union. Until this point, the Conservative Party was the only major British political party without a written constitution. This absence had allowed the leadership to maintain its dominance of the party, denying rights to the membership. In a sequel to the sleaze of the Major government, Jonathan Aitken was imprisoned in 1999, having been convicted of perjury. This stemmed from a dishonest libel action by Aitken, who challenged reports of his receiving financial inducements from

Saudi Arabian businessmen, which led to his departure from the Cabinet in 1995.

Labour carried the National Minimum Wage Act in 1998, a measure that the Conservatives opposed. The Blair government also founded Sure Start, and improved the National Health Service. Following approval in referendums, held in the respective nations during 1997, the Scottish Parliament and Welsh Assembly were set up in 1999. These bodies successfully implemented a measure of self-government for Scotland and, to a lesser extent, Wales, which continues to develop. There were also major changes in the political situation in Northern Ireland, and the virtual ending of terrorist violence in the province – a positive contrast to Tory Unionist sectarianism. The changes followed from the Belfast Agreement (generally known as the Good Friday agreement) reached between the governments of Britain and the Republic of Ireland, in April 1998. The agreement was approved the following month, in separate referendums, in both Northern Ireland and the Republic of Ireland. The Northern Ireland Assembly was created in 1999, and began to take responsibility for devolved government, bringing together Catholics and Protestants. The House of Lords Act 1999, passed after some resistance by Conservatives, removed the hereditary peers, apart from a group of 92 members, whose position in the Lords was maintained by their winning a ballot amongst themselves.

The Human Rights Act 1998, incorporating the European Convention on Human Rights into British law, was a fine achievement of the Labour government, but the Conservative focus lay elsewhere. During that year, Augusto Pinochet, the former Fascist dictator of Chile, was arrested on a visit to Britain, and held under house arrest, pending possible extradition to Spain, to face trial for crimes committed by his regime. In 1999, Margaret Thatcher made a speech – to a fringe meeting – at the Conservative Party conference, for the first time since her downfall as Prime Minister, calling for the release of Pinochet. Thatcher celebrated the actions of Pinochet's Fascist dictatorship, claiming that it had built a "prosperous democratic order". Thatcher failed to mention that Pinochet had ordered the murder of countless thousands of people. Thatcher also visited Pinochet, who she described as a friend. After a protracted legal battle, Pinochet was released in 2000, and allowed to return to Chile, on the questionable grounds that he was too frail to face a trial.

The Conservatives won the European Union election held in June 1999, with 36 seats ahead of Labour's 29, while the Liberal Democrats took 10 seats, and the others 12. Nevertheless Hague was held in low esteem by much of the general public. Michael Portillo, a member of the Major government, who lost his seat at the 1997 General Election, was returned to the Commons, in a By-Election at the end of 1999. Portillo was given a prominent role in the Shadow Cabinet by Hague in early 2000, and appeared to be a possible rival. Another shadow from the past arrived later in the year, as Jeffrey Archer was charged with committing perjury in his 1987 libel case, and promptly suspended from the Conservative Party by Hague. Archer was subsequently tried, convicted, and imprisoned. Part of the trial coincided with a General Election campaign, with polling on June 7 2001. Labour won another landslide, with 413 seats, and a majority of 167. The Conservatives returned 166 MPs, a gain of just one compared with the 1997 Election, while the Liberal Democrats took 52 seats, and the others 28.

William Hague immediately announced his resignation as Conservative Leader, and the process to replace him started, with ballots among the party's MPs held in July. After three rounds, Kenneth Clarke and Iain Duncan Smith eliminated Michael Portillo, David Davis, and Michael Ancram. The top two in the MPs' poll went forward to a contest in which party members had a vote, with Iain Duncan Smith winning by 61 per cent to Clarke's 39 per cent, when the result was announced in September. Duncan Smith was helped by an announcement of support from Margaret Thatcher, who favoured his Eurosceptic line, whereas Clarke had long been an enthusiast for the development of the European Union.

IDS, as he became widely known, had been elected to Parliament 1992, and joined the Conservative front bench after the 1997 Election defeat. He was the first Roman Catholic to lead the Conservative Party. Duncan Smith proved to be a weak Leader, whose authority rapidly declined. He sacked David Davis from the role of Party Chairman, and appointed Theresa May, in July 2002. May was the first woman chair of the Conservatives, but they did not think to rename the post as Chairperson. A few months later, May told the Conservative Party Conference "There's a lot we need to do in this party of ours. Our base is too narrow and so, occasionally, are our sympathies. You know what some people call us? The Nasty Party". The phrase "Nasty Party" was increasingly used by opponents of the Conservatives over the next few years. During 2003, Duncan Smith was troubled by the "Betsygate" scandal, being accused of improper use of public money in paying his wife, Betsy, to work as his diary secretary. A Parliamentary investigation concluded Duncan Smith had not broken the rules, but he and Betsy appeared to have benefitted from some confusion.

On October 29 2003, Duncan Smith lost a vote of confidence among Conservative MPs, by a margin of 90 to 75. Michael Howard became the next Leader, elected unopposed on November 6. Howard, who had served in government under Thatcher and Major from 1990 to 1997, was an improvement compared to Duncan Smith. Tony Blair's reputation was now damaged by the perception that his government had exchanged clarity for the tales of its "spin doctors". The government's handling of the Iraq war, in the Spring of 2003, and its aftermath, particularly undermined Blair's standing. The case for participation in the war hinged on the claim that the Iraqi regime, led by Saddam Hussein, was readily able to deploy weapons of mass destruction. It soon became clear that Blair had exaggerated the extent of the threat, and Michael Howard made an impact, leading Conservative pressure on the government. In June 2004, the Conservatives managed an unconvincing victory in the European Union election, with 27 per cent of the vote. The Conservatives won 27 seats, Labour 19, UKIP 12, the Liberal Democrats 12, and the others 8.

14 We Are All in This Together

Labour defeated the Conservatives, in a third successive General Election, on May 5 2005, obtaining a majority of 66. Labour won 356 seats, the Conservatives 198, the Liberal Democrats 62, and the others 30. The day after the Election, Michael Howard announced his decision to stand down as Conservative Leader. Following a review of the rules for Leadership elections, which did not lead to any changes, a contest began in October. Two ballots led to David Cameron and David Davis advancing, while Liam Fox and Kenneth Clarke were eliminated. The vote among party members saw Cameron defeat Davis by 68 per cent to 32 per cent. Cameron – educated at Eton and caught smoking cannabis there – had only been an MP since 2001. He struggled to establish a strong image as Leader, being criticised by many for his relative inexperience, and faced difficulty uniting the party. A veneer of socially-conscious Conservatism alienated the right, despite Cameron's clear Euroscepticism.

Tony Blair stepped down as Prime Minister in 2007, and was replaced by Gordon Brown, the new Labour Leader, who had been Chancellor of the Exchequer for a decade. Brown faced the onset of an international financial crisis, which intensified during 2008, becoming a global recession. This was the biggest failure of capitalism since the depression of the 1930s. Brown, and the Labour government, spent vast amounts of public money to rescue private sector banks. Blaming Labour for events beyond their control, Cameron and the Conservatives gained ground. In June 2009, the Conservatives won the European Union election, with 25 seats, while UKIP took 13 seats, Labour 13, the Liberal Democrats 11, and the others 10. The Conservatives resumed their link with the Ulster Unionists, running a joint campaign in the Northern Ireland section of this election.

Public confidence in the British political system was severely reduced by the scandal of MPs making excessive, often illegal, claims for expenses. After requests under the Freedom of

Information Act had been blocked, due to lengthy resistance by MPs, the *Daily Telegraph* leaked information, during 2009. The newspaper largely used the expenses detail against the Labour Party, and in favour of the Conservatives. Being outside the public sector, the *Daily Telegraph* was exempt from Freedom of Information, and did not have to disclose how much, and to whom, it paid for the leaked detail. It subsequently transpired that the *Telegraph* bought the information for £150,000 from John Wick, a supporter of the Conservative Party, with former links to the security services. The deal was agreed by Will Lewis, editor of the *Telegraph*, who moved the following year to News International.

The electoral pact between the Conservatives and Ulster Unionists experienced an embarrassing rejection, as Sylvia Hermon, the only sitting Ulster Unionist MP, resigned from that party in March 2010. The Unionist alliance failed to win any seats at the subsequent General Election, and the pact was soon discontinued. That Election, held on May 6 2010, led to a hung Parliament, with the Conservatives having 307 seats, Labour 258, the Liberal Democrats 57, and the others 28. The Conservative Party had failed to win a majority for a fourth successive General Election – their worst sequence of results since the six successive defeats between 1847 and 1868. After several days of negotiations between parties, Gordon Brown and the Labour government departed from office, being replaced by a Conservative and Liberal Democrat coalition. David Cameron became the Prime Minister, while Nick Clegg was his Deputy – a Con-Dem double act. Cameron, aged 43, was the youngest Prime Minister since Lord Liverpool, a Tory, who took office in 1812.

The Coalition quickly set about massive public spending cuts, with the Conservatives using a budget deficit as an excuse to attack public services. Cameron and the government told people "we are all in this together", but the continuing problems of recession, aggravated by austerity, had a disproportionate impact on people with lower incomes, while the Conservatives rewarded rich people with massive tax cuts. The policy was overseen by George Osborne, a complacent Chancellor of the Exchequer, who had inherited a multi-million pound fortune. Unemployment increased to almost 2,700,000 people by the end of 2011 – the highest figure since 1994. The Coalition government inherited a national debt of £960 billion, when it was formed in 2010, and proceeded to make the situation worse. From 2015, a solely Conservative government's continued mismanagement of the economy led to the National Debt reaching £1,786 billion at the end of 2017 – an 86 per cent rise in seven and a half years. Annual interest payments on the National Debt were £48 billion in 2017. The position continued to worsen, and the National Debt reached £2,004 billion in July 2020 – with debt exceeding the UK's annual gross domestic product for the first time since 1961.

A messy compromise between the Conservatives, who opposed electoral reform, and the Liberal Democrats, long in favour of some reform, led to a referendum on the generally unsatisfactory Alternative Vote, in May 2011. The electorate rejected AV by 68 per cent to 32 per cent, a result which damaged the cause of reform. Later that year, the Coalition carried the Fixed Term Parliament Act, setting a five year duration for the legislature – unless there was a vote of no confidence in the government, or a majority vote of two thirds of MPs in favour of an early General Election. The main motive was a wish, by the government, to bind the two parties making up the alliance, with a law that would force them to remain together, in power.

The Health and Social Care Act 2012 led to major reorganisation of the National Health Service, the following year, with the Conservatives undermining the service through fragmentation and privatisation. Dozens of the Conservative MPs who voted for the legislation benefitted financially, through links to private health companies, which won contracts as parts of the NHS were sold off. The Welfare Reform Act 2012 unfairly disadvantaged many benefit claimants, particularly with the introduction of an under-occupancy penalty, generally known as the Bedroom Tax. Major cuts to Legal Aid were also imposed. The Conservatives were regularly reminded of the "nasty party" tag by the Labour Party, led by Ed Miliband, who replaced Gordon Brown in 2010.

The Conservative Party, along with their friends in UKIP, whipped up hysteria about immigration, undermining Britain's multi-cultural society. Internal argument among Conservatives over Britain's role in the European Union continued to influence the leadership. At the start of 2013, David Cameron announced that a referendum on British membership of the EU would be held, if the Conservatives won the next General Election. The death of Margaret Thatcher, in April 2013, led to re-assessment of her legacy. While Conservatives lauded Thatcher as a saviour of Britain, many people saw that Thatcher had encouraged a form of capitalism that was in crisis, sold off important public assets, and divided the nation. A lasting effect of Thatcher's policies was a drop in the level of support for the Conservatives, who only gained a majority in one out of the five General Elections between 1992 and 2010. In the Summer of 2013, the Coalition government's plan for armed intervention in the civil war in Syria was defeated, in a vote by the House of Commons, as the Labour Party led the argument against this course. Cameron, who misjudged the situation, pledged that the government accepted the will of Parliament.

In May 2014, the Conservatives were reduced to third place in the European Union election, with 19 seats. UKIP won the election with 24 seats ahead of Labour, who took 20 seats. The Liberal Democrats were left with a single MEP, while the other parties won 9 seats. After a protracted and damaging trial, Andy Coulson, formerly director of communications for David Cameron, was convicted of previously organising phone-hacking at the *News of the World* – part of the News International group – and sent to prison, in July 2014. Cameron's judgment in appointing Coulson, who had already been under suspicion, was questioned. July brought another scandal, with allegations that Conservative MPs were active in a paedophile ring, during the Thatcher administration, prompting Theresa May, the Home Secretary, to announce an inquiry into historic allegations of child sexual abuse. The chair of the enquiry, Baroness Elizabeth Butler-Sloss, had to step down a few days after her appointment, due to public pressure, as her brother, Michael Havers, had been Attorney General in the Thatcher government. Following this May blundered again, appointing Dame Fiona Woolf, who also resigned as chair, due to her friendship with Leon Brittan, who was accused of suppressing a dossier about paedophile MPs in 1984, when he had been Home Secretary.

An independence referendum was held in Scotland, on the initiative of the Scottish National Party administration. In the weeks leading up to polling, in September 2014, the Conservatives were worried that the outcome would be a vote for independence. With the Tories and Liberal Democrats unpopular in Scotland, the government was reduced to leaving much of the detailed campaigning against independence to the Labour Party, with Gordon Brown taking centre-stage. The referendum rejected independence, at this point, by a margin of 55 per cent to 45 per cent. The government committed British forces to take part in air strikes against the Islamic State terrorists in Iraq, having received backing from the House of Commons, in September. Meanwhile direct British military activity in Afghanistan reached an end, 13 years after the 2001 intervention, led by the USA, started under Tony Blair's government. Some British forces, however, remained to provide non-combat support to the Afghan army.

During the Autumn, two sitting Conservative MPs, Douglas Carswell and Mark Reckless, defected to UKIP, and were returned to Parliament for the latter party, at By-Elections. Nigel Farage, the reckless UKIP Leader, fanned fruitless speculation about other MPs defecting from the Conservative Party – which he had once been a member of. Many people were concerned about the openly racist, xenophobic, sexist, and homophobic comments regularly made by prominent members of UKIP. Besides a cynical approach to Europe, UKIP had an extreme outlook, bordering on Fascism. In 2006, Cameron said "UKIP is sort of a bunch of fruitcakes and loonies and closet racists". After ruling out a Conservative pact with UKIP across several years, Cameron changed his mind in Autumn 2014. There was growing support among members of the Conservative Party and UKIP for the idea that, in the event of another hung Parliament, right wing parties should work together. In late 2014, and the early part of 2015, Liberal Democrat members of the government, anticipating the forthcoming General Election, sought to distance themselves from the Conservatives. There was clear evidence that the Coalition was failing to deal effectively with the budget deficit, and national debt. The Coalition reorganisation of the NHS had left it in crisis, and the Labour Party's rescue plan was growing in popularity.

15 Coalition of Chaos

A General Election was held on May 7 2015. Opinion polls pointed to a repeat of the 2010 hung Parliament, but the Conservative Party unexpectedly won a majority, for the first time since 1992. The Conservatives took 331 seats, ahead of Labour with 232 seats, while the Scottish National Party returned 56 MPs, the Liberal Democrats 8, and the others 23. The SNP took all apart from three of the seats in Scotland, with 40 of their gains being from Labour. The Lib Dems lost 27 seats to the Conservatives, their former coalition ally. UKIP accumulated 3,881,129 votes, but were left with only one MP, Douglas Carswell. The Conservative majority, of 12 seats, was won with only 37 per cent of the votes cast. There were a lot of scare tactics during the campaign. Theresa May, Home Secretary in the Con-Dem coalition, claimed that the emergence of a possible minority Labour government, backed by the Scottish National Party, would be the biggest constitutional crisis in Britain since the Abdication of Edward VIII in 1936.

A major reason for the Conservative victory emerged in the following months. Numerous police forces investigated the Conservative Party over alleged fraud, on the basis of clear evidence that campaigning expenses at the General Election were not declared in line with the law. Expensive campaigning in around 30 marginal constituencies, won by the Conservatives, was not declared as an expense in those constituencies, being instead reported as part of their national campaign. Conservative strategists had worked out a deliberate plan to win marginals, with a large budget from party headquarters. Known as the Tory Election Fraud, this was cheating on a scale not seen since the Rotten Boroughs of the nineteenth century. Conservative MPs elected through this scheme started to worry about prosecution, and disqualification from Parliament.

The success of the 2015 marginals campaign masked a major problem within the Conservative Party, that of falling membership. The party continued to be largely financed by corporate donations, with speculative hedge funds increasingly prominent. This paid for expensive advertising at General Elections, but the party was lacking large groups of activists, able to win the political argument, at constituency level and on a level playing field. From a peak of 2,800,000 in 1953, Conservative Party membership gradually reduced over the next few decades, and dropped below 1,000,000 in the 1980s, during Thatcher's premiership. The decline became more pronounced, with membership shrinking to 150,000 at the end of 2013. Thereafter the Conservative leadership refused calls to issue updates. In 2017, membership was generally estimated by outside commentators to be around 100,000. By contrast, 570,000 people were members of the Labour Party. Among the British citizens who had decided to fully engage in the political process, Labour led the Conservatives by a ratio of over five to one.

The leaking of the "Panama Papers", covering the international scandal of tax havens, in April 2016, damaged the Conservatives. Besides the party's failure in government to effectively regulate tax schemes in British overseas territories, there was specific detail of several wealthy Conservatives making financial gain. These included David Cameron, who inherited a fortune from his late father, part of which was built up by Blairmore Holdings, a company registered in Panama back in 1982 – taking advantage of the abolition of exchange controls by the Thatcher government. Blairmore was run by British investors, but did not pay any British tax on its profits. Despite being caught benefitting from tax avoidance, Cameron refused to resign as Prime Minister.

During protracted negotiations with the European Union, Cameron failed to achieve the significantly improved deal, for Britain, he indicated was possible. He announced, in February 2016, that the Referendum on membership would be held on June 23 that year. Left arguments against multinational capitalism, along with the primacy of EU legislation over British law, were overwhelmed by the xenophobia of UKIP, and a large part of the Conservative Party. Cameron held the referendum to appease the Tory right, believing he could end their dalliance with UKIP. Through most of the campaign the mainstream media, and opinion polls, pointed to a vote to remain in the EU. During the early hours of June 24, the results were declared, and it gradually became clear that the British people had voted to leave the EU, with the final margin being 52 per cent to 48 per cent. Probably the major reason for the vote in favour of Brexit was the suggestion, by the Vote Leave campaign, led by Tory MPs, that the UK's gross contribution to the EU, £350 million per week, could soon provide extra funding for the NHS. Brexiteers did not address the fact that about half the gross contribution to the EU was returned to the UK, providing major support to agriculture and regional development. Cameron said during the campaign that, if the referendum voted for leave, he would promptly invoke Article 50 – the relevant provision of the EU Treaty of Lisbon 2007 – and oversee the withdrawal process. This statement was proved to be a lie, only an hour after the referendum result was known. Abdicating responsibility, Cameron immediately announced his plan to resign as Prime Minister. Cameron left Parliament a few months later, and went on to a lucrative career, lobbying Conservative ministers on behalf of big business.

Five candidates participated in the Conservative Party Leadership contest. They did not, however, include Boris Johnson, one of the figureheads of the Vote Leave campaign in the Referendum. Johnson had only become a convert to the Leave cause in February 2016, apparently as an opportunist vehicle for opposing Cameron as leader. With Michael Gove, the Justice Secretary – also prominent in Vote Leave – launching his own Leadership bid with a scathing attack on Johnson, the latter dropped a planned candidature. The first ballot eliminated Liam Fox, while Stephen Crabb withdrew. The next vote eliminated Gove, leaving Theresa May and Andrea Leadsom as the two MPs who would progress to the ballot of party members. A few days later Leadsom withdrew, having made insensitive personal comments about May. Suddenly Theresa May was Leader of "the nasty party", and appointed as Prime Minister, by Elizabeth II, on July 13.

May now delivered a speech in Downing Street, pointing out some of the inequalities in British society, but forgetting to mention the role of the Conservatives in causing problems which she now offered to solve. May concluded by saying "We will make Britain a country that works not for a privileged few, but for every one of us. That will be the mission of the government I lead, and together we will build a better Britain". Thereafter May's government signally failed to honour this pledge, preferring instead to continue the harsh austerity, and other divisive policies, pioneered by Cameron. Within weeks, there was a setback for May, as Dame Lowell Goddard became the third chair of the child sexual abuse inquiry to resign – each of these chairs had been appointed by May when she was Home Secretary. With several other senior participants in the process also departing, in acrimonious circumstances, over the next few months, while groups representing victims of abuse expressed a lack of confidence in the process, no tangible progress was made.

Theresa May became premier with a mantra of "Brexit Means Brexit", but would not say when Article 50 would be invoked to actually start the two year process of Britain leaving the European Union. During several months of confusion, the government clearly lacked a plan, and rumours of back-tracking increased. There was a successful legal challenge to the government's claim that Article 50 could be invoked by Royal Prerogative, and specific legislation had to carried before the decision was formally notified to the European Union, in March 2017.

A snap General Election followed on June 8, after May won a vote, in the House of Commons, to over-ride the Fixed Term Parliament Act timetable. May, who had consistently denied suggestions that she would call an early Election, now asked for a personal mandate for Brexit. May said that, if she lost her majority, responsibility for negotiations with the EU would pass to Jeremy Corbyn, a radical Socialist, elected Labour leader in 2015. At the start of the General Election campaign, the Crown Prosecution Service decided not to prosecute the MPs, and agents, accused in the Tory Election Fraud, on the ridiculous ground that it was not in the public interest for the courts to decide whether the previous Election had been stolen by the Conservatives. It appeared the establishment had decided upon a cover up.

May tried a presidential-type campaign, focused on herself rather than her party, but failed to engage with the public – most of her meetings being restricted to Conservative members and supporters. In a television interview, May was asked to recall the naughtiest thing she had done as a child. May said "I have to confess, me and my friends, sort of, used to run through the fields of wheat, the farmers weren't too pleased about that". May was widely ridiculed for the anecdote. When challenged by a nurse, during a televised debate, about restrictions to pay, May said "We will put more money into the NHS, but there isn't a magic money tree that we can shake that suddenly provides for everything that people want". May, and the Conservatives, banged on about their offer of "Strong and stable government". They contrasted this with the "Coalition of chaos", envisaged if the small Conservative majority was replaced by a progressive government led by Labour, with support from the SNP, Plaid Cymru, and the Green Party. The Conservatives also consistently smeared Jeremy Corbyn, saying his dialogue with Sinn Fein – which eventually helped the Good Friday peace agreement for Northern Ireland in 1998 – equated support for IRA terrorism. The Conservatives were reduced to 318 seats, losing their majority, as Labour made gains, emerging with 262 MPs. Meanwhile the Scottish National Party won 35 seats, the Liberal Democrats 12, the Democratic Unionist Party 10, and the others 13.

May, forgetting that loss of her majority should open the way for a government led by Corbyn, desperately sought an alternative arrangement on the morning after polling day. The weak and wobbly May decided to cling on to power, leading a minority Conservative government, in an unholy Parliamentary alliance with their "friends", the Democratic Unionist Party. The regressive DUP opposed gay marriage and abortion, but supported creationism being taught in schools. May backed up the deal with a major increase in central government funding for Northern Ireland, having suddenly found the "magic money tree". The DUP had long-standing links with loyalist terrorist organisations, including the Ulster Volunteer Force, the successor to the Conservative and Unionist militia. In the years from 1910 to 1914, the Tories argued there was no mandate for the Liberal government's programme, as they were a minority administration, kept in power by the support of Irish Nationalist MPs. A century later, May thought the backing of a group of Irish MPs was a reasonable way for a minority Conservative government to stay in power. May cried wolf in 2015 over the constitution, and plunged Britain into crisis during 2017. The Conservative and DUP agreement conflicted with the legal responsibility of a British government to be neutral in dealings with the Northern Ireland parties, in line with the Good Friday Agreement. With the governance of Northern Ireland in limbo, following the collapse of a DUP and Sinn Fein administration earlier in the year, this had major implications. The Conservative and DUP "Coalition of chaos" proved to be a nightmare for the nation.

A fire at Grenfell Tower, a multi-story block of flats in Kensington, London, caused the deaths of 72 people, a few days after the General Election. May, along with the Conservative-controlled Royal Borough of Kensington and Chelsea council, pledged to re-house people within weeks, but months later a large number of the former residents of Grenfell were living in temporary accommodation. There were many other failures. Boris Johnson, the Foreign Secretary, continued to make the discredited claim that £350 million per week could be saved by Brexit, and transferred to the NHS. Jeremy Hunt, Secretary of

State for Health, blundered through an escalating crisis, and encouraged rapidly increasing privatisation of contracts. In the Autumn of 2017, Hunt told the Conservative Party Conference: "Nye Bevan deserves credit for founding the NHS in 1948, but that wasn't him or indeed any Labour minister. That was the Conservative health minister in 1944, Sir Henry Willink, whose White Paper announced the setting up of the NHS". Many people smelt a rat, or at least a large piece of fake news. Hunt's ludicrous claim failed to deal with the fact that the party's MPs, including Willink, voted against the Labour legislation that set up the service.

In the final weeks of 2017, allegations of sexual misconduct led to the dismissal from the Cabinet of Michael Fallon, the Defence Secretary, and Damian Green, effectively the Deputy Prime Minister. A "Tory Sex Pest" list, compiled by staff working for Conservative MPs, was leaked to the media. The list, featuring 36 MPs, contained allegations of sexual impropriety by some of them, along with rumoured examples of poor taste by other honorable members, engaged in consenting acts with their colleagues. It was reported that Gavin Williamson, the Conservative Chief Whip, provided regular briefings to May on misconduct among Tory MPs, with this being used in the process of party management – a polite term for blackmail. Priti Patel, Secretary of State for International Development, also departed, having had clandestine meetings with members of the government of Israel.

At the start of 2018, May tried to revive her government, with a reshuffle, but this failed to meet its objective. There were strong rumours of plotting, by opportunistic Conservatives, to remove May from the leadership. May, who was constantly indecisive, repeated the callous nature of Thatcher, but with a lack of competence. An increasingly vitriolic split between Brexiters and Remainers, about the way forward for the minority Conservative government, showed the true nature of the nasty party. A "Hostile Environment", directed by Conservative governments, from 2010 onwards, towards illegal immigrants spilled over into racist mistreatment of legal migrants. The revelations of the Windrush Scandal showed that many people who arrived from Caribbean islands, decades earlier, were having their British citizenship removed. Amber Rudd was forced to resign as Home Secretary, in April 2018, having mishandled the issue, but a lot of the blame lay with May, who directed the policy during her tenure in that role.

Brexit negotiations with the European Union made little progress, during a series of crises for May, and her government. Opponents of Brexit issued dire warnings about risks to the future strength of the nation. The campaign for Brexit, during the referendum, spoke about taking back control of the British economy and law-making process. In contrast to these laudable aims, there was a strong undercurrent of xenophobia among some elements of the Brexit project. There were major concerns that a lack of clarity about the future links between Northern Ireland and the Republic of Ireland – including a possible "hard border" – could undermine the success of the peace process. David Davis, the Brexit Secretary, and Boris Johnson, the Foreign Secretary, both resigned from the Cabinet in July 2018, as they disagreed with their colleagues' strategy.

Theresa May finally reached a withdrawal agreement with the EU in November 2018, the detail of which prompted the resignation of Dominic Raab, who had only replaced Davis as Brexit Secretary four months earlier. In the government reshuffle, Amber Rudd returned to the Cabinet, only seven months after her Windrush disgrace. The government failed to comply with a resolution of the House of Commons, instructing them to issue the legal advice they received on the withdrawal agreement. On December 4, a further resolution found government ministers to be in contempt of Parliament – an unprecedented rebuke. A week later, May unilaterally postponed a Commons vote on the withdrawal agreement, following three days of debate, admitting that her government would have been defeated. Brexit-supporting Conservative MPs forced a possible vote of no confidence in May as Leader of the party. Jacob

Rees-Mogg, an advocate of hard Brexit, from the backbenches, known for his outdated opinions, and nostalgia for a pre-democratic age, had recently emerged as a surprise possible Leader. The vote was held on December 12, with May winning by 200 votes to 117, after offering to stand down prior to the next General Election, but over a third of the Tory MPs had tried to bring her down immediately.

As the year 2019 began, six years after David Cameron had announced the referendum plan, and three years after he set the date of that vote, his successors in a Conservative government were failing to deal with the national crisis of a potential "no deal Brexit". The date of the United Kingdom leaving the European Union had been set in law, as March 29, but there was no certainty as to what would happen then, and thereafter. The delayed vote on the withdrawal agreement arrived on January 15, amidst high drama, as the House of Commons inflicted a crushing defeat on May, rejecting her deal by 432 votes to 202. The 230 vote defeat for the government was unparalleled in British political history. Jeremy Corbyn immediately announced that he was tabling a vote of no confidence in May's government. That motion was defeated the following day, by a margin of 325 to 306, with May only avoiding defeat due to the votes of DUP MPs.

May brought back her Brexit deal on March 12, and it was defeated in the Commons by 391 votes to 242 – a massive margin of 149 votes. May reluctantly agreed a short Article 50 extension, with the rest of the EU, having been directed to do so by Parliament, thereby reneging on her frequent assurances that Brexit would take place on March 29. Instead that date saw May's third Commons defeat on the withdrawal agreement, by 344 votes to 286 – the scale of rejection being reduced to 58 votes. During April, May was again forced to accept a delay to Brexit, offered by the EU, this time until the end of October 2019 (if a deal was not ratified earlier than that date), to prevent an immediate departure without a deal. The United Kingdom participated in elections to the EU Parliament, held in late May, and Theresa May announced a protracted timetable for her departure as Prime Minister. The Conservatives only won four out of the 73 UK seats in the EU election, with just nine per cent of the popular vote. On both measures, the Conservatives finished in fifth place, behind the Brexit Party, Liberal Democrats, Labour, and Green Party. The Brexit Party had recently been set up by Nigel Farage, who had broken with the declining UKIP.

16 Take it on the Chin

In March 2019, a new One Nation Conservatives group was set up, quickly attracting the membership of dozens of MPs. The aim was to unite against a supporter of a hard Brexit replacing Theresa May, as Prime Minister, in anticipation of a Tory Leadership contest. Party membership had suddenly risen to 160,000 people, partly due to defectors arriving from UKIP, attempting to bolster Brexit. Boris Johnson and Jeremy Hunt reached the final stage – a year after the former had been replaced as Foreign Secretary by the latter. At the start of July, Nicky Morgan and Nicholas Soames, both senior backbenchers, wrote a letter on behalf of the One Nation group, asking Johnson and Hunt about their Brexit plans. Johnson's reply expressed his wish "to make it absolutely clear that I am not attracted to arcane procedures such as the prorogation of Parliament". There was speculation that prorogation might be planned, as a way to prevent Parliament blocking a no deal Brexit. Johnson defeated Hunt, by a margin of 66 per cent to 34 per cent, in the ballot of party members.

Johnson was appointed Prime Minister, on July 24, with an untested assurance, for the queen, that he commanded a majority in the House of Commons. Johnson was widely distrusted, due to his serial dishonesty and incompetence, plus racist, sexist, and homophobic comments. Most members of the previous Cabinet, including May and Hunt, immediately departed, either refusing to serve under Johnson, or being sacked. Johnson favoured hardline Brexiteers, including Priti Patel, who became Home Secretary, less than two years after leaving May's government in disgrace. Dominic Cummings, the supposed mastermind of Vote Leave in 2016, was appointed as chief advisor by Johnson. May's government had failed to deliver an exit from the EU, three years after the referendum, but Johnson claimed departure would happen on October 31, a date three months away, with or without a deal.

Alexander Boris de Pfeffel Johnson was born in the USA, during 1964, the son of Stanley Johnson, a man destined to become a Conservative MEP. During an education at Eton College and Oxford University, the privileged Boris Johnson displayed a lazy attitude to his studies. Johnson was a member of the notorious Bullingdon Club at Oxford, along with David Cameron. As a journalist, Johnson was sacked by the *Times*, in 1988, for making up a quote. He became MP for Henley in 2001, on the retirement of Michael Heseltine, and stood down in 2008, upon becoming Mayor of London. During 2004, Johnson published *Seventy Two Virgins*, a racist novel, and was sacked from the Shadow Cabinet for lying – dishonestly denying an affair. Womanising and infidelity has been a common thread in the Johnson story, including his infamous affair with Jennifer Arcuri, a businesswoman from the USA, who supposedly gave him technology lessons, during his tenure as Mayor of London. That role ended in 2016, the year after Johnson returned to the Commons, as MP for Uxbridge and South Ruislip. Throughout his career as a journalist and politician, Johnson has cultivated an image as a buffoon, but he regularly makes offensive comments – often followed by flippant attempts at apology. Examples include Johnson referring to black people as "piccaninnies" with "watermelon smiles", suggesting that Islamic women wearing burqas "go around looking like letter boxes", while gay men were derided as "tank-topped bum boys". Johnson's misguided admirers in the Conservative Party often refer to his being "socially liberal", but there is a lot of evidence to the contrary.

Jacob Rees-Mogg, as Leader of the House of Commons, obtained the questionable agreement from the monarch – on August 28 2019 – to prorogue Parliament, for five weeks, leading up to a planned Queen's Speech in mid-October. This was only a few weeks after Johnson's letter to One Nation MPs, saying he would not prorogue Parliament. In defiance of the Tories' long-prized constitutional convention, the government were seeking to prevent Parliamentary scrutiny of Brexit plans, and legal challenges began. Johnson's rationale, "the whole September session is a rigmarole introduced by girly swot Cameron to show the public that MPs were earning their crust", was a truly ridiculous thing for a Prime Minister to write in an official government memo.

In early September, Parliament passed what was known as the Benn Act – introduced by Hilary Benn, a Labour MP, and son of Tony – requiring Johnson to seek a further extension to Brexit if, by October 19, Parliament had not approved either a withdrawal agreement or a no deal departure. Boris Johnson withdrew the whip from 21 Conservative MPs, who voted to facilitate Parliament debating the Benn legislation. These included Nicholas Soames, a grandson of Winston Churchill. Nicky Morgan, the other One Nation leader supposedly concerned about Johnson's Brexit plans, had strangely joined his government when it was formed, and was rewarded for her loyalty to him with a peerage, at the start of 2020. The punishment of 21 colleagues prompted the resignation of two Cabinet Ministers, Jo Johnson (brother of the Prime Minister) and Amber Rudd. The combined Conservative and Democratic Unionist Party MPs were now in a minority position in the Commons. Johnson, acting with increasing irrationality, said "I'd rather be dead in a ditch", when asked if he would seek a Brexit extension. Johnson, Gove, and other ministers, floated the possibility that the government might simply ignore the law. In late September, after Parliament had been prorogued for two weeks, the Supreme Court ruled the event unlawful, and the legislature resumed sitting.

Parliament sat on a Saturday (for the first time since the Falklands War, 37 years earlier), the date being October 19, to consider an amended agreement, which Johnson had reached with the EU. The Commons voted to delay any approval until the necessary legislation had been passed. Johnson sent the letter to the EU, required by the Benn Act, but petulantly refused to sign it, and also dispatched a contradictory argument against an extension. Three days later, the Commons gave a Second

Reading to the Withdrawal Agreement Bill, but rejected a government attempt to rush it through Parliament. Johnson announced a pause in this legislative process, and was forced to agree with the EU that Brexit would be delayed for a third time, probably until the end of January 2020. When the extension was in place, Johnson got the agreement of the House of Commons, at the fourth attempt, to an early General Election. With the polling date set as December 12 2019, Britain entered its first Winter Election since February 1974 – and the first such contest in December since 1923.

At the start of the campaign, the government suppressed release of a report, from the House of Commons Intelligence and Security Committee, on growing interference in British politics by Russia, including large scale funding of the Conservative Party by Russian oligarchs – it finally arrived the following Summer. The Conservatives sought to make Brexit the main Election issue, and were helped by the Brexit Party not opposing sitting Conservative MPs. Labour proposed a programme to end austerity, and rebuild the NHS plus other public services. Labour aimed to negotiate an improved deal with the EU, and put this to a second referendum, with an option to remain rather than leave.

When the results were announced, the Conservatives won 365 seats, and a majority of 80. Labour were reduced to 203 MPs, their worst total since 1935, largely due to the loss of support in areas that voted to leave the EU. The SNP took 48 seats, the Liberal Democrats 11, the Democratic Unionist Party 8, Sinn Fein 7, and the others 8. Despite great proclamations from Farage, who lacked the courage to actually stand as a candidate, the Brexit Party failed to win any seats. Many people feared what would occur under a right wing Conservative government, with a programme more extreme than the Thatcherism of the 1980s. Johnson aimed that Brexit would be followed by a trade deal with the USA, which could open up the NHS to increased privatisation. The Conservatives also planned changes to the legal and political structure of Britain, that would curb opposition to the government. When the new Parliament opened, Johnson's government reintroduced the EU Withdrawal Agreement Bill. It became law eight days before the United Kingdom left the European Union, the latter event taking place on January 31 2020. This ended the era of EEC / EU membership, which had lasted 47 years, and the UK entered a transition period, due to expire at the end of 2020.

The first UK cases of the Covid-19 Coronavirus pandemic were diagnosed on the day that Brexit took place. Johnson and his government, particularly Matt Hancock, the Health Secretary, took little action to alert the public to the scale of the danger. Johnson announced, on March 3, "I was at a hospital the other night, where I think a few there were actually Coronavirus patients, and I shook hands with everybody, you'll be pleased to know, and I continue to shake hands". Johnson's handshakes were politeness turned into pure irresponsibility. The government, and some scientific advisors, favoured the idea of attempting to create "Herd Immunity", with Johnson saying in a national television interview "one of the theories is that perhaps you could take it on the chin, take it all in one go and allow the disease, as it were, to move through the population, without taking as many draconian measures". Laymen pointed out the massive number of deaths that would be likely in Britain, before the remainder of the population could hope for "Herd Immunity". The government backed down, but the strategy remained far from clear.

The Cheltenham Festival horse race meeting went ahead as usual – allegedly due to gambling companies lobbying the government against possible cancellation – with crowds of around 60,000 people per day, something that was soon shown to have spread Covid. Other sports events were postponed, upon the decision of organising bodies, rather than government direction. The response of Johnson was complacent, until pressure from NHS staff, opposition parties, scientists, and the wider public, prompted action, as the death toll rose. The government belatedly started to recommend social distancing, and closed schools. Johnson did not announce the much-delayed effective lockdown until March 23.

Hancock had declared the NHS to be ready for the spread of the illness, back in January. In the following months, testimony from clinicians, and patients, showed this was not true. Hospitals that were struggling, due to underfunding during a decade of austerity, suddenly had to deal with additional admissions of Covid patients. There was a shortage of ventilators, despite claims by the government that they were urgently arranging to increase production and acquisition. Many frontline health workers lacked the required Personal Protective Equipment (PPE). The UK rapidly suffered one of the largest Covid death totals, per head of population, in the world, and this continued to be the case for many months. The government placed support of the capitalist economy, and big business – the natural plus financial friends of the Tories – ahead of the need to save lives, and protect the wider community.

In late May, it was revealed that Dominic Cummings and his wife, Mary Wakefield, had deliberately broken lockdown, while both ill with Covid, taking a trip from London to Durham. Wakefield and Cummings also published a false account, claiming that they stayed in London, self-isolating, while unwell. Despite widespread public anger, and political pressure, Johnson refused to dismiss Cummings. A few months later, Cummings departed from his role, having upset Carrie Symonds, who was Johnson's partner, and a person with a disproportionately large influence in a power struggle within Downing Street. Lockdown eased over the late Spring and Summer, with pubs and restaurants re-opening, and then schools returned to normal in September. These events caused a rise in Covid cases, to which Johnson and his government reacted with a delayed second lockdown, lasting four weeks, from early November to the start of December. Post-Brexit negotiations, between the UK government and the EU, took place at intervals during the transition period, with increasing concern that unrealistic demands from Johnson's team could prevent a trade deal. An agreement was finally announced on Christmas Eve, following which Parliament approved legislation on December 30, and the European Union (Future Relationship) Act 2020 received Royal Assent on the last day of a tumultuous year.

Johnson announced a third lockdown, on January 4 2021, as the numbers of Covid cases, and deaths, moved towards a peak higher than in the first wave, the previous Spring. On January 26, with over 100,000 people having died from Covid, Johnson told a press conference "I am deeply sorry for every life that has been lost and, of course, as I was Prime Minister I take full responsibility for everything that the government has done. What I can tell you is that we truly did everything we could, and continue to do everything that we can, to minimise loss of life and to minimise suffering in what has been a very, very difficult stage, and a very, very difficult crisis for our country, and we will continue to do that". Johnson's claim that "we truly did everything we could" was not supported by the facts. Throughout the pandemic, the government displayed a grotesque combination of incompetence and corruption. Co-ordination of the national Covid Test and Trace system was outsourced to Serco, a private company, rather than being led by the NHS. The head of Test and Trace was Dido Harding, a Tory peer. Edward Argar, one of the Conservative Health ministers, was a former executive at Serco. The current chief executive of the company, Rupert Soames, was the brother of Nicholas Soames, who had recently retired as an MP. The test and trace programme failed to be effective, despite a massive budget, which increased to £37 billion in March 2021. The government also awarded hundreds of multi-million pound contracts to private companies, for the procurement of PPE. Many contracts went to organisations, with little or no experience in PPE, run by people who were donors to the Conservatives, or friends of the party's MPs. In an attempt to conceal the extent of the PPE scandal, Matt Hancock delayed publication of the contracts, which led to a High Court ruling, during February 2021, that he had acted unlawfully.

Dominic Cummings gave evidence to a House of Commons Select Committee, investigating the national response to Covid, at the end of May 2021. Cummings was very critical of both Johnson and Hancock, for their failures to address the severity of the situation. Cummings said that, during the Spring of 2020, Hancock had been dishonestly telling government ministers, and advisors, that hospital patients would not be discharged to care homes unless they had been tested for Covid. Hancock denied the allegation of misleading colleagues, but it was a matter of public record that many thousands of people were discharged without testing, in March and April 2020. This almost certainly led to thousands of avoidable deaths, as Covid spread among elderly and vulnerable people in care homes.

In an attempt at distraction, a few days after Cummings gave evidence, Johnson suddenly got married, for the third time. His new wife, Carrie Symonds, had a brief role as head of communications for the Conservative Party, in 2017 and 2018, which ended under a cloud – there were allegations that Symonds submitted incorrect expenses claims. Covid restrictions were gradually eased in the Spring of 2021, while Johnson's government continued to give mixed messages. Border control had been haphazard throughout the pandemic, and there was now a delay of several weeks in restricting travel from India, where Covid cases were particularly high, as Johnson sought a trade deal with the authoritarian government of that state. This led to a large number of British cases of the Delta Variant, first identified in India. On June 14, Johnson was forced to announce that the end of restrictions on social gatherings, planned for a week later, would be delayed.

At the end of June, it emerged that Matt Hancock was having an affair with Gina Coladangelo, a long-term friend, who had been appointed a director at the Department of Health and Social Care a few months earlier. Johnson declined to sack Hancock, accepting the latter's apology for breaking workplace social distancing rules, with video from CCTV in Hancock's office showing him kissing Coladangelo. Amidst much criticism for his latest Covid-related failure, Hancock resigned from the government, the day after Johnson failed to dismiss him. The incoming Health Secretary was Sajid Javid, a former investment banker, with no experience in the field of health. Javid had been appointed Chancellor of the Exchequer when Johnson became Prime Minister, but departed from the role in early 2020, following a clash with Cummings. On July 5, Johnson announced the end of Covid restrictions would happen a fortnight later, despite his acknowledgement that new cases were rising fast. Javid supported this reckless move. The Covid death total in the UK was now 128,000 people, based on the government's preferred measure, which was a death within 28 days of a positive test. A more accurate record showed that over 152,000 people had Covid mentioned as a cause on their death certificate. Johnson's mantra was "Build Back Better", as he spoke of post-Covid economic revival, but the evidence from 11 years of Conservative government, since 2010, was not promising.

David Cameron, Theresa May, and Boris Johnson were each portrayed by supporters as modern Conservatives, in touch with ordinary people. The reality was a continuation of established themes, which had motivated their party since its foundation in 1830. For nearly two centuries, the Conservative Party has been run by a wealthy and powerful minority, motivated by their narrow self-interest. For most people, Britain has been a poorer place, both morally and financially, as a result of Conservative politics.